CELEBRATING AT HOME

CELEBRATING AT HOME

prayers and liturgies for families

DEBORAH ALBERSWERTH PAYDEN AND LAURA LOVING

UNITED CHURCH PRESS
CLEVELAND, OHIO

United Church Press, Cleveland, Ohio 44115
© 1998 by Deborah Alberswerth Payden and Laura Loving

Biblical quotations are from the New Revised Standard Version of the Bible, © 1989 by the Division of Christian Education of the National Council of the Churches of Christ in the U.S.A., and are used by permission. Adaptations have been made for clarity and inclusiveness.

Printed in the United States of America on acid-free paper
03   02   01   00   99   98   5   4   3   2   1

Library of Congress Cataloging-in-Publication Data
Payden, Deborah Alberswerth, 1953–
    Celebrating at home : prayers and liturgies for families /
Deborah Alberswerth Payden and Laura Loving.
        p.   cm.
    Includes bibliographical references.
    ISBN 0-8298-1250-4 (pbk. : alk. paper)
        1. Family—Prayer-books and devotions—English.   I. Loving, Laura,
1951–   .   II. Title.
BV255.P38   1998
249—dc21   97-44100
                                                                              CIP

. . . .

To my parents, Roy and Vi Alberswerth, who handed on to me the stories and traditions of faith, home, and family;

To my husband, Tom, for his calm reassurance and poetic soul; and to his parents, Anna and Neal, for nurturing him;

To my daughters, Anna and Rachel, who remind me always of the importance of celebration;

To the members of First Congregational United Church of Christ, South Milwaukee, Wisconsin, who, in sharing their joys and struggles, compelled me to write this book;

To all those known and unknown saints who surround me with their creative presence;

I give thanks to God for you.

—Debbie

To the red-tailed hawks, who have taught me about mindfulness.

—Laura

. . . .

CONTENTS

· · · · · · · ·

AN INVITATION   IX

MAKING SENSE OF LIFE   X

FOR EVERYTHING THERE IS A SEASON   XI

AND A TIME FOR EVERY MATTER UNDER HEAVEN   XII

CHRIST CANDLE   1

SABBATH   3

    Sabbath as Day of Rest   3

    Sabbath as Mindfulness   5

PRAYERS FOR DAILY LIFE   7

    Mealtime   7

    Bedtime   8

    Anytime   9

    Morning and Evening   10

    Spontaneous Prayers   16

    Times of Waiting   18

    Receiving Bad News   19

    Reconciliation   19

SEASONS OF THE CHURCH YEAR   21

    Advent   21

        Saint Nicholas Day   24

        Saint Lucia Day   26

        Las Posadas   34

    Christmas   38

        Kwanzaa   42

    Epiphany   44

    Mardi Gras/Shrove Tuesday   48

    Lent   51

        Ash Wednesday   52

        Palm Sunday   54

        Holy Week   55

        Maundy Thursday and Good Friday   56

        Holy Saturday   59

    Easter   60

    Pentecost   64

    Common Time   67

        Trinity Sunday   67

        Reformation Sunday   68

Contents

All Saints' Day   70

Harvest and Thanksgiving Celebrations   74

Reign of Christ Sunday   78

SEASONAL CELEBRATIONS   80

New Year's Eve and New Year's Day   80

Martin Luther King Jr. Day   84

Valentine's Day   85

Saint Patrick's Day   87

Mother's Day   88

Festival of the Christian Home   89

Memorial Day   89

Father's Day   92

Fourth of July   93

Labor Day   95

Beginning of the School Year   96

Travel and Vacations   99

LIFE TRANSITIONS   103

Birth   103

Adoption   105

Birthday   106

Confirmation   109

La Quinceañera   111

Graduation   113

Wedding   114

Wedding Anniversary   115

Blessing for a New Home   116

Moving   118

Divorce   120

Times of Vocational Change   122

Hospitalization and Treatment   126

Extended Caregiving   129

Death   133

A TIME TO MOURN AND A TIME TO DANCE   135

LIST YOUR FAVORITES AND WRITE YOUR OWN   136

GOODBYE—GO WITH GOD—AND REMEMBER WHO YOU ARE!   139

ADDITIONAL RESOURCES   140

AN INVITATION

. . . .

Welcome, welcome!
Come in. Come in and join us!
Stay a while. Sit a spell.
Set the table. Decorate the room.
Light a candle. Read the Scripture.
Say a prayer. Sing a song.
Laugh out loud. Shed your tears.
Dance a jig. Be still and listen.
Join hands and celebrate being God's people!
This is what we offer you.

We offer this book to you as a gift. It is designed to be used in your daily living, seasonal celebrations, and times of transition. It provides prayers, blessings, scripture readings, liturgies, and ideas to be used in your home to celebrate being God's people. There are resources to use during the church year and during transitional times in your personal life.

This recipe book is not complete. It is not meant to be. It is a beginning point. We put it together from our perspective, experiences, and love of ritual and tradition. Add your own family and ethnic traditions and rituals. Bring out the Bible and hymnal. Mix in old and new family stories. Stir in your favorite food and drink. Bring out the old family recipes or try new ones. Embellish with your creativity. Invite children and elders, family and friends, to join you. We invite you to use this book as a resource for celebrating the life of faith in your home. Enjoy!

MAKING SENSE OF LIFE

Life is confusing. It is too often chaotic and hectic. Seasons come and go. Life changes around us. It is easy to forget what it means to be God's people. We yearn to have order and make sense out of our living. We yearn to be in touch with something greater than ourselves. We yearn for ritual and tradition. We hunger for God.

Ritual and prayer put us in touch with the transcendent nature of the Divine. Time set aside for ritual and tradition gives us sanctuary from daily struggles and routine. The words, symbols, and actions of rituals provide tangible ways of expressing the intangible mystery of life and death. We are able to act out what is of ultimate value in our lives. Traditions connect us to our history and give direction to our present and future. Ritual and tradition help us to interpret the meaning and purpose of life. Celebrations move us through times of change and transition. They offer a perspective about life's journey. Ritual and tradition help to form our identity as God's people. They tell us who we are and what God intends for us.

Home is the first place that we are taught the Christian faith. It is the soil in which the first seeds of discipleship are planted. Martin Luther called the home "the domestic church." Providing times of ritual, prayer, and tradition in the home is essential to our formation as Christian disciples. Home prayers and liturgies do not replace the importance of participating in the life of a local church. We are a communal people of faith, not isolated Christians. Home celebration and worship strengthen the mission of the larger church. Home and church work together to nurture our identity as disciples of Christ.

FOR EVERYTHING THERE IS A SEASON

. . . .

The yearly changes of the natural seasons help us to mark time. There is a rhythm to these changes in nature. Each season in this cycle brings with it certain ways of living. Yearly holidays give us pause to take time out of our routine and celebrate.

The Christian church year provides us with a framework for understanding who we are as a community of believers. There are a rhythm and a rhyme to the yearly flow of church seasons. They walk us through the life and ministry of Jesus Christ, and call us to discipleship in today's world.

Our biblical ancestors had a set order of scriptures read for each Sabbath worship and festivals throughout the year. The scriptures and seasons of celebration reminded them of their history as God's people. The years were marked off by the cycle of sacred time. The repetition enabled them to form their identity as God's people as they moved through history. In hearing the Word of God and reenacting the events from salvation history, our ancestors rehearsed that history and became a part of it.

The Christian church adapted and transformed the cycle to celebrate the good news of Christ. Each church season—Advent, Christmas, Epiphany, Lent, Easter, and Common Time—is filled with particular stories, songs, images, colors, and festivals. They teach and remind us of the ministry of Jesus. Centering our lives on the church year is a powerful reminder of our identity as disciples of Christ. From Sunday to Sunday, day in and day out, from season to season, from holy day to holy day, we are called to be God's people.

AND A TIME FOR EVERY MATTER UNDER HEAVEN

Along with the traditional church season and festivals, there are significant times of transition in our lives. Some of these transitions happen on a yearly basis. Others occur only occasionally, while still others happen only once in a lifetime. These occasions of transition and accomplishment are important to recognize. We cannot forget that God's presence is with us in all of these events. We need to set aside opportunities to affirm an individual's gifts and achievements, to celebrate the joys of life, and to accept the struggles and disappointments we face. In doing so, we recognize the presence of God in all times in our lives. We offer to God our thanksgiving for the gifts we have received. We ask God's guidance and healing in facing the brokenness of life. Ritual and tradition, liturgy and prayer, song and story, help us to put our lives in perspective—God's perspective.

> It is good to give thanks to God,
> to sing praises to the Most High;
> to declare your steadfast love in the morning,
> and your faithfulness by night.
> (Psalm 92:1–2)

CHRIST CANDLE

· · · · · · · · · · ·

Our faith tradition has long used symbols. Symbols provide a concrete way of pointing to a greater reality of the faith. One of the central symbols of both Jewish and Christian faiths is that of light. The symbol of light reminds us of God's power and presence. Candles are most often used for this light symbol. Candles in worship suggest the presence of God through Christ in our midst, as well as recalling that Christ is the Light of the world. Some churches have a special Christ candle, which displays a Christ symbol such as a Chi-Rho (☧) or an Alpha and Omega (A Ω).

Besides being used in congregational settings, candles are important symbols in our homes. Jewish families begin their weekly Sabbath observance by lighting candles. Christians use candles at baptism and during Advent and Christmas to serve as reminders of God's presence. Other times of transition, such as birthdays, marriages, anniversaries, and graduations, also call for candles.

We suggest that families have a Christ candle for their homes. Such a candle can be lit each Sunday as a reminder of the Christian Sabbath Day. It can also be used throughout the year for special celebrations and rituals as a reminder of Christ's presence in our lives. Throughout this book, you will find suggestions for using a Christ candle.

You can purchase a Christ candle in almost any church supply store. A large white pillar candle works best, but a tall white taper may meet your needs. Or you can make your own Christ candle. One way to do that is to roll sheets of white beeswax to form a thick candle.

You can put a Christ symbol on your candle in several ways. "Draw" a Christ symbol with glue and sprinkle gold glitter over it, then shake off the excess glitter. Cut your symbol from gold foil paper and glue it to the candle. An alternative is to cut a Christ symbol from a sheet of yellow beeswax. Attach it to the candle by brushing the back of the design with hot wax and pressing it onto the candle. Or hold the beeswax design against the candle as you blow air over it with a hair dryer turned on low, and press the design gently with your hands until it sticks. Symbols such as a cross, Chi-Rho, fish, or cross and crown work well. Consult a Christian symbols book for other ideas.

Consider making a Christ candle a yearly family activity. Create one at the start of the Christian new year (Advent) or for Easter Sunday. As with all flames, be careful lighting and using your Christ candle, particularly with children.

After you have made or purchased your candle, say the following blessing as you light it for the first time.

CHRIST CANDLE BLESSING

Source of all illumination, may this candle be a reminder of your presence in our midst. May we light it knowing that in its glow we are blessed by your grace and everlasting love. May the light of Christ that shines forth from this candle be reflected in our daily lives. Come, Holy Giver of light and life, celebrate with us and guide us in our journey of faith. Amen.

SABBATH

· · · · · · ·

Sabbath as Day of Rest

"So God blessed the seventh day and hallowed it, because on it God rested from all the work that God had done in creation" (Gen. 2:3).

In its most elemental form, Sabbath is setting aside a regular and intentional time to honor God and focus on the centrality of the faith in our lives. It is easy to forget in our busyness that our vocation in life is to be disciples of Christ. The values and pressures of society can too easily seduce us into thinking otherwise. We are called to be people of faith, a faith centered in communal worship of God and care of one another.

Sunday is "resurrection day." It is the first day of the new week. It is the day we recall the gift of life that God has given to us in Jesus Christ. It is a day of new creation, a day of new beginnings. It is a day set apart to honor God for all that God has done for us. Therefore, Sunday begins with worship.

Sunday has traditionally been Sabbath Day. The Christian life is centered in communal worship. Each week begins for us as we gather in our local churches to offer praise to God in song, story, sermon, scripture, and prayer. The weekly centering and proclamation with our brothers and sisters of faith remind us of who we are and what God expects of us in this world.

Sabbath is also a time to refrain from the routine of work. We can too easily be consumed by the hectic pace and necessity of daily work and responsibilities. We live in a world where our lives are often defined by our busyness and the product of our work. But even God rested after the work of creation. Made in God's image, we are called to a time of intentional rest and re-creation.

Too often, Sunday has become a day cluttered with work. It becomes difficult for us to detach ourselves from business responsibilities. We need a time of structured respite from our daily routines. Weekly Sabbath rest can rejuvenate our spirits, help to put life into perspective, and focus us on the joy of being part of God's creation. Our faith proclaims that keeping a regular Sabbath Day to honor our Creator, and to rest and be refreshed, is of value in our lives.

Begin each new week in your household by celebrating Sabbath. Begin the day by lighting a Christ candle. Attend worship together. Talk on the way home about your experience of the teaching, preaching, and serving ministry in your church that day. Discuss over dinner what is taking place elsewhere in the life of your congregation and how your household will be involved in it. Look over the upcoming week and what it holds for each member around the table.

Take time to relax, play, and be together as a family. Read a book, go to a movie, play games, engage in a family project, take a bike ride, or visit friends together. Honor God this day by your presence in communal worship and by your presence with one another.

PRAYER FOR SABBATH DAY (SUNDAY)

(Begin your Sabbath/Sunday by lighting your Christ candle. Have it lit in the morning as people awake and begin the day.)

Blessed are you, O God of Sabbath. Make us mindful this day of the greatness of your creation. Remind us what it means to be your people. May we be renewed by the hearing of your Word. May we find rest from the weariness and routine of our daily work lives. Restore our identity as your people. Refresh our hearts, minds, and spirits for the days ahead. Re-create us in your divine image. We ask this Sabbath prayer in the name of the one whose resurrection we celebrate every day of our lives, Jesus the Christ. Amen.

Sabbath as Mindfulness

The subject of Sabbath is usually considered only when the conversation turns to the Ten Commandments. But the topic is larger than the plaster tablets we remember from church school days. When Sabbath becomes a part of our daily mentality, we have a better idea of what was intended for this holy rest.

The best description of Sabbath we have ever heard came from the wisdom of a youth in confirmation class. When asked what "Remember the Sabbath and keep it holy" meant, Andy responded, "God says, 'Don't forget me!'" What an appropriate way to think of Sabbath—as a memory of God. This response to God's request can happen in many ways.

Mindfulness is a form of Sabbath. Not limited to a particular day of the week or holy place, mindfulness is a way of being attentive to the holiness of God. Paying attention to one's breathing, to the taste and texture of breakfast, to the sacramental rhythm of schedules, to the shimmer of asphalt or the blades of grass—all of these exercises in mindfulness honor God's presence in details. Family members may need to start slowly, practicing mindfulness in stages. You may want to ask one another at dinner, "What made you mindful of God today?" You may start an evening bedtime prayer with the question, "What were your Sabbath moments today?" As you practice this discipline, you will find Sabbath seeping into all the nooks and crannies of your life. Sabbath will surprise you.

Another form of Sabbath intends this element of surprise. It is modeled after Mountain Day, a venerable tradition at Smith College. One fine day in October, the president of the college awoke to proclaim amnesty for the entire campus. The college bells pealed from the hilltop, and Mountain Day officially began. Classes were canceled. The president glided through the library shooing the too-serious scholars out of musty carrels and into the azure and gold fall day.

Students took long hikes in the mountains, played monotonous games of Monopoly, sprawled on the banks of Paradise Pond, and rested from the rigors of academic routine. Perhaps you can declare Mountain Day early one Saturday morning and leave behind the mountain of chores, choosing instead to head for the beach, take a family hike in the woods, or ride the city bus all around town. Open your senses to the presence of God. Thank God for the freedom to break out of the ordinary and into the extraordinary. Maybe you think you cannot afford a whole day for this mountaintop experience. Then return to the first suggestion and take the smaller steps of mindfulness before you attack the serendipity of mountain climbing.

Try to observe the larger purpose of the tradition of remembering God by setting aside time, space, and intent for the sole purpose of honoring God. You will be surprised by the many ways that Sabbath can be observed. Write some of your own Sabbath discoveries below, and refer to this page when your well runs dry and you are ready for refreshment.

_____

_____

_____

_____

_____

_____

_____

_____

_____

_____

_____

_____

_____

_____

PRAYERS FOR DAILY LIFE

· · · · · · · · · · · · · · · · ·

Taking time to pray on a daily basis reminds us of the One to whom we belong and on whom we rely for life. Mealtime and bedtime are two traditional times for families to pray. It does not matter whether daily prayers are traditional or new blessings, or daily ones created by family members, or whether they are sung, said, or silent. What is important is to take intentional time to pray each day to the Source of our being and blessings.

Mealtime

Prayers at mealtime may be spoken or silent. The emphasis is on the acknowledgment that all gifts come from God. When Laura's family used to go around the circle and say a simple thank-you for gifts of the day, her youngest son, Nathan, would start out, "I'm thank you for . . ." Each of us is a thank-you to God, a gift given back in gratitude. Try some of these prayer ideas. Use a traditional table grace or add your own to this collection.

God, we call upon your name. Creator of the universe, we thank you for this food from the earth. Lover of justice, we pray for all who hunger for food and for justice. Deep Well of life, refresh us at this table. Amen.

– or –

Ask each person to name one thing in this day for which to give thanks. Join hands and at the conclusion of the thank-you prayers, one person says:

Thank you, God, for all of these hints of you in our day. Hear our prayers of gratitude. Make us mindful of all your blessings as we eat at this table together. Amen.

— or —

Observe a period of silence before a meal. Hold hands and squeeze the next hand as your silent prayer is offered to God. When the circle is complete, raise your joined hands above your heads and say together, Amen!

Bedtime

As the day closes and night enfolds us, prayers before going to sleep can put the day into perspective. Quiet time prayers can relax us, center us, and permit us to reflect on the joys and struggles of the day. Since the night can sometimes be fearful, prayers before sleeping can help us remember that God's presence is always near. Songs and lullabies work well as part of a bedtime ritual.

A BEDTIME LITURGY

Child: Thank you, God, for this day.

Parent: *(Recall two or three things from the day for which you are grateful.)*

Child: *(Name two or three people for whom you will pray; lift up joys, concerns, worries, and thanks.)*

Parent: Bless us through the night, and help us to wake refreshed and ready to serve you. Amen.

— or —

(Light a candle for this prayer and extinguish it as you say "Amen":)

Pray: Comforter God, erase the shadows from the walls, the fears from our minds, the weariness from our bones. Merciful God, forgive us for all we have left undone, for all we have done that we should not have done, for all the mistakes of the day. Now send us into sleep to restore our spirits, to renew our energy, and to wake clear-eyed and full of your praises. Amen.

Anytime

Every day we experience events and situations that call for prayer. Prayers of thanksgiving and joy, prayers for help, prayers of confession, and petitions on behalf of others can be said anytime and anyplace. They can be simple one-line supplications or praise prayers. Here are a few samples of times for prayer:

••• After learning to ride a bike: "O God, we have a prayer of joy that Peter learned to ride a bike today."

••• Upon seeing a night sky full of stars: "O God, how beautiful are the stars in heaven!"

••• When someone is hurt: "Sarah hurt her arm today playing. Help her arm to heal, O God."

These one- or two-line prayers help us to be mindful in our daily lives that the wonders of God's creation are all around us and God's presence is always near.

Morning and Evening

These prayers for bracketing the day can be as simple or elaborate as you choose. Each daily prayer time suggests a theme. You may wish to keep some objects handy to set the tone for the daily theme. Use a cardboard carton and cover it with a collage or decoupage of pictures denoting gratitude and/or prayerfulness, scenes of family life, or nature photographs. A wicker basket or wooden bowl could also be the receptacle for your worship materials. Keep it simple and have fun collecting, preparing, and changing the symbols or icons. Each day the suggested contents from the prayer box are designated in parentheses. Pencil in your own ideas.

SUNDAY MORNING: MEDITATE ON THE WORD
(Objects: open Bible, Christ candle, _____)
You may have the lectionary readings ready for today and choose to read one or all of the selections. Light the Christ candle before you read, and extinguish it at the close of the prayer. You may say aloud a psalm fragment about God's Word and wisdom (e.g., Ps. 1:1–2; 19:7–11; 71:15–16; 75:1; 92:1–3; 111), or choose your favorite passages from the Psalms. Conclude with this prayer or one like it:

O Wisdom, we get our nourishment from you. You feed us with imagery and poetry. You refresh us with promise and presence. Every day we hear new truths in your Word. Inspire us to act with the courage of the prophets and the compassion of the disciples. Fill us with the tender morsels of your wisdom that we might go to the hillsides and the markets, the classroom and the congregation, and feed those who are hungry. Thank you, we are full. Amen.

SUNDAY EVENING: REPOSE

(Objects: hymnal, church bulletin from today's worship, recorded music and a cassette player, _____)

If possible, choose one of the hymns that you sang in worship this morning, and sing it tonight. If you cannot do this, meditate on the text of the hymn together. You may also wish to play meditative music to create a quiet circle of space.

Read: *(Read Psalm 84:1–7 or Psalm 139:1–12 or the psalm of the day in the lectionary.)*

Pray: **You are our resting place, O God. We put to rest this day the songs and sermon, the remnants of Sabbath. We rest in the knowledge that you know us and care for us. You hear our solo voices and our whispered prayers as well as the four-part songs and corporate prayers of the congregation. Thank you for loving us as we are and for nurturing and nudging us to grow in wisdom and faith. Thank you for the community of faith, which sustains us and challenges us. Hear us as we breathe our prayers of sleep, resting in you. Amen.**

MONDAY MORNING: RISE AND SHINE

(Objects: cymbals, noisemakers, a toy trumpet—or a real one!—small bell, pots and pans, _____)

Read: *(Read Psalm 150.)*
            Parade around the house making a joyful noise!

Pray: **Holy One, Mighty God, you have called us to this day. You have called us out of bed, out of sleep, out of dreams. You have called us to make a joyful noise. Help us to make that noise wherever we go today. Let the sound of cymbals and crashing pot lids follow us through the corridors and highways and tunnels and valleys of our day. Send us on our way rejoicing. Amen!**

MONDAY EVENING: COMFORT AND GRACE
(Objects: bird's nest, feathers, remnant of a "retired" baby blanket, pieces for a patchwork quilt, a small pillow, _____)

Pray: **Now the day is over. We made a lot of noise today. Some of it was about you. Some of it had no meaning. Still our voices now. Grace us with your quiet presence. Soothe us with your soft voice. Wrap us in your comfort. Amen.**

Sing: "Amazing Grace," "All Through the Night," "Now the Day Is Over," or some other evening lullaby.

TUESDAY MORNING: MINDFULNESS
(Objects: candle, egg timer, magnifying glass, _____)
Today you will focus on being mindful of your surroundings, of the sacredness of small tasks. You will listen when a child speaks. You will note the bird in flight. You will savor your food.

This prayer of attentiveness will be with you throughout the day:

You are here, God, in the midst of things. In the smallness, in the silence, in the flurry and the noise. You are here, God. And I am with you. Amen.

Turn over the egg timer or set a kitchen timer for three minutes, and allow yourselves the luxury of looking or listening, smelling, tasting, touching. Pray through your senses in silence. When the timer goes off or the sand has sifted to the bottom, get up and begin a day of mindfulness.

TUESDAY EVENING: INTERCESSION
(Objects: photographs of friends, relatives; newspaper or magazine pictures of people in various life situations; address book, Christmas card list, bundle of Christmas cards received last year; _____)
Remembering people in need of prayer is another form of practicing mindfulness. Tonight after supper, take out some of the pictures or old Christmas cards that you have stored in the worship box. Read the Christmas letters. (C'mon, you can do it.) Celebrate the good news; commiserate with the tough luck. Offer prayers for the folks in the letters, the pictures, or your address book. You may want to pray something like this:

Helper of the lost, help *(names)*.
Giver of new life, watch over *(names)*.
Weaver of friendships, keep us connected to *(names)*, etc. Amen.

WEDNESDAY MORNING: BALANCE

*(Objects: small narrow rectangle of lightweight wood, a small triangle for a
fulcrum, _____)*
Wednesday is often thought of as the hump day—something to get over
to get to the rest of the week. Try reframing it as the fulcrum day, a day of
balance, of open-mindedness, of considering alternatives, weighing ideas,
and measuring actions in light of their justice factor. Set up the teeter-
totter you have constructed out of lightweight wood.

Pray: **O God, in Christ you have shown us a balance: righteous
indignation tempered with tender compassion, stillness
and Sabbath-mind focused by action and intentionality,
knowledge informed by common sense and grace. Create
in us a sense of balance today. Give us clean hearts and
new spirits. Steady us for our day lived in Christlike pre-
cariousness. Amen.**

WEDNESDAY EVENING: REFLECTION

*(Objects: Christ candle, shallow bowl to be filled with water, mirror and
stones, shells, sand in a plastic lid or box top, _____)*

Read: *(Read Psalm 23.)*

Pour water into the basin. Reflect on the still waters of your day. What
were the valleys? How did your cup overflow? Where was the Shepherd
present? Introduce these metaphors from the familiar psalm as a way of
reflecting on your life. Study the reflection of the Christ candle in the
bowl of water, letting the image calm your mind. Close this evening's
meditation by reciting or reading the psalm together.

THURSDAY MORNING: BEACON
(Objects: kerosene lamp, flashlight, Christ candle, _____)

Read: *(Read Matthew 5:14–16.)*

Discuss, children and adults alike, what you can do to be a beacon today. Make a commitment with one another to be the lamp on the hill in a specific way. Check in later in the day to see how it is going and to offer encouragement or congratulations.

Pray: **Shine through us, O Light. Let your goodness filter through us into the shadowed nooks and crannies of the world. Find your way into the folds of our hearts, too, and open us to the bright light of forgiveness and freedom. We pray in the name of the One who sets us free, Jesus Christ. Amen.**

THURSDAY EVENING: COMMUNION OF SAINTS
(Objects: Christ candle, icons, photographs, _____)

You may wish to use some of the photographs from Tuesday evening's collection, or you may alternate as the weeks go by and you remember people before God. Children may enjoy a whimsical approach to creating a community of saints—by stuffing clothes to look like people and propping them up at the table with you. These life-sized figures are reminders of the larger community outside your household. You may also light the Christ candle and place it in the center of the table with the photographs displayed around it. Christ is at the center of this circle.

Pray: **God of the ages, we remember those who have gone before us. We recall their courage and their faith. God of the human family, we pray for our sisters and brothers who are celebrating or suffering, who are fighting famine, who are studying, who are learning to walk, who are giving birth, who are facing death. We especially remember *(names)*. Bind us together in one human community, that we might all be one. Amen.**

FRIDAY MORNING: TAKING OURSELVES LIGHTLY

(Objects: feather, fan, _____)

Breathe in slowly, and exhale. How many times will you do that today without thinking? Turn on a fan, blow on a feather, watch the wind in the trees, or listen for a whisper. It is a day for taking it easy, for taking ourselves lightly, and for enjoying the Spirit's dance through our lives.

Pray: **Spirit, breathe through us today. Fill our hearts with laughter. Open our eyes to wonder. Speak to us in the wind and in the whisper of prayer. Help us to breathe new life into old projects, to revive tired relationships, to sit still and listen. Help us to breathe in the aroma of coffee brewing or bread baking or the familiar smell of home. Help us to sweeten life for people who struggle. Soar in us and make all things possible. Amen.**

FRIDAY EVENING: SHABBAT SHALOM

(Objects: cutout Stars of David, prayer shawl (if available) to be used as a table covering, Hebrew Bible, candles,_____)

This is a night of standing in solidarity with our Jewish brothers and sisters as they light the Sabbath candles. You may light candles too, and read from the Hebrew Scriptures. If a prayer shawl is available, drape it over the table. Suggested readings: Deuteronomy 6:4–9 (the Shema), Exodus 20:1–17 (the Ten Commandments), Psalm 111 (a Psalm of Praise). Your family might want to attend services at a synogogue or temple. Ask the rabbi to share an evening Sabbath prayer that your family might use at home. Or sit together and write a prayer for Sabbath peace. Younger children might want to draw their images of a peaceful night. Close with the Hebrew words for Sabbath peace: Shabbat Shalom!

SATURDAY MORNING: CO-CREATORS WITH GOD
(Objects: clay, small building blocks, yarn, beeswax, origami paper,
_____)

For some families, Saturday is a play day. Playing is not just for children. Get involved with the creative process somehow this morning. Read together from the opening verses of Genesis, or just sit without reading and create something together. God delights in the creative spirit. These creations are as precious as prayers. Whether you end up with an origami crane or a lopsided play-dough pot, leave it as a centerpiece on your table, a symbol witnessing to the Creator in your midst. Try a different medium each week. You will be surprised at your creativity even if art anxiety has you in its grip!

SATURDAY EVENING: CLEANSING
(Objects: bubbles, _____)

Is it myth or reality that the family used to line up for the Saturday night bath to get ready for church? You may not be pouring water into a metal washtub, but a bath can be a ritual of cleansing and preparing. Before you get down to the nitty-gritty, though, play and pray together. Get out the bubble wands and bottle, and swirl soap bubbles around the kitchen, run them across the lawn, send them sailing out the window, or silently christen someone with a gentle, wafting, iridescent orb. Playfulness is a part of sacred ritual. You may wish to let the dance of bubbles be a prayer in itself, or you may want to close the evening with a traditional prayer. Either way, your words and wishes will find their way to the One who hears and delights in us.

Spontaneous Prayers

Medieval times were filled with the sound of the Angelus, the bells of the cathedral that announced the hours of prayer. Upon hearing the bells, people would stop their work in the fields and kneel down to pray. Perhaps we can relabel some of our contemporary realities to transform them into Angelus moments.

There are moments in family life that call for prayer but do not allow for ceremony. One of these moments is a time when sirens pierce the air as rescue units rush past. Here are some suggestions for short prayers to be used at this time. They may help you grow into using spontaneous prayers no matter what is happening.

Pray: **O God, the eerie sound of the siren calls us to prayer. Give courage to those who are summoned to help. Be present with those who are in need. Comfort those who are frightened. Send your healing power and your compassionate care in this time of crisis. Amen.**

— or —

Pray: **Healer, be present. Presence, be swift. Guardian, grant safety. Grant all your gift. Amen.**

— or —

Pray: **Strengthen those who use their strength to help others. Listen with those who strain to hear a heartbeat. Blow your breath into those who struggle for air. Wrap your love around those who are scared. Comfort those who grieve. We pray in Christ's name. Amen.**

— or —

Chant: The family may wish to respond with a chant. While this may sound as if it belongs in the lofty choir stalls of a cathedral, it is actually quite an accessible spiritual discipline. The phrases are simple, and repetition is the key to this ancient practice. [*You may find chants from the Taizé community in France* (e.g., Jesus, remember me, Ubi Caritas, O Lord, hear my prayer) *in the service music of your hymnal. Or you may order Taizé chants from GIA Publications in Chicago, at 1-800-GIA-1358.*]

Times of Waiting

Waiting is often one of the most difficult activities in our lives. Waiting makes us feel as if we have no power to resolve the situation at hand. We feel helpless and at times hopeless. We like to be able to take control and change the situations in which we find ourselves. But our times of waiting need not be empty times. Prayer is a way to fill the void of waiting. Prayer is "doing something" in times of waiting. Praying is a way of being actively engaged in the situation at hand. Here are two suggestions for prayer during times of waiting.

We are trying to be still and know that you are God.
We are trying to keep faith and know that you are at the helm.
But we are afraid. Be a centerboard for our little boat as we sail off into uncharted seas.
Be a rudder for us. Steady us. Calm us. Amen.

— or —

A Breath Prayer Litany for Times of Waiting
(Times of awaiting test results, looking for a loved one to return home in bad weather, working through labor pains, or anticipating important news by phone or mail.)

One Voice: Tick.
Other Voice: Tock.
Unison: Tick, tock, tick, tock.
One Voice: With each moment we are counting.
Other Voice: In each moment we are waiting.
Unison: In this moment we will breathe in your Spirit, O God.

(Take several slow, deep breaths, and create room for the compassionate Spirit to fill you.)

Receiving Bad News

(Light the Christ candle.)

One Voice: In life and in death we belong to God.
All: O God, you are our beginning and our end. We look to you
                    for comfort. Be with us as we deal with the changes and the
                    challenges of grief. Help us to start our day with you, even
                    when we feel alone. Help us to end our day with you, even
                    when our burdens seem too heavy to bear.
One Voice: In life and in death we belong to God.
All: Thanks be to God! Amen.

Reconciliation

Arguments are part of daily life in households. Sometimes arguments and squabbles just die a natural death. Other times they are resolved through a negotiated peacekeeping agreement, a time-out, or enforced separation of the "warring parties." If you have a designated time-out, call the family members together again for a brief, but formalized reconciliation.

Read: *(Read Psalm 133:1.)*

Have a family member say one of the following prayers:

God of the whirlwind, grant us stillness now. We have been thrown off course by our arguing and our power struggles. Help us to know that you love us as we try to love one another. We pray in Christ's name. Amen.

— or —

Forgive us, God, for our fighting. You have created us to be instruments of your peace. Help us to stay in tune with your plan for us. Amen.

— or —

Dear God, we have said some things that make us cringe as the words echo in our memories. Clear the air. Clear our minds. Move us into the next step together that we might live in peace together. Amen.

— or —

LITANY OF RECONCILIATION

One Voice: For bitter words said in haste or anger;
Others: We are sorry, God.
One Voice: For listening for faults instead of imagining possibilities;
Others: Forgive us, God.
One Voice: Smooth the rough places
Others: And make us mindful of your presence.
One Voice: Heal us and hear us.
Others: Amen.

— or —

Pray: O Peace, O Holy One, O Comforter,
             we have wounded you as we have hurt one another.
             Help us to treat each other with love and respect.
             For you are the peace at our center, the holiness in our
             midst, the comfort we need. Amen.

SEASONS OF THE CHURCH YEAR

Advent

The church year begins with the season of Advent. "Advent" means "coming." Advent begins on the fourth Sunday from the beginning of Christmas. (Count back four Sundays from December 25 and that is the beginning of Advent.) Advent is a time to prepare ourselves both internally and externally for the coming of Christ into our lives. We prepare to celebrate the birth of Jesus so long ago, and we consider what it means for Christ to enter into our lives today. Advent is a time of hope. The prophetic words of hope given to ancient Israel are still relevant today. In a world that often seems too violent and despairing, the hope of Advent is needed like water for a thirsty plant.

Purple is the traditional liturgical color for Advent. It symbolizes repentance as well as royalty. In recent times blue has replaced purple in some churches, to mark Advent as a more joyous season.

Children seem to have difficulty separating Christmas from Advent, particularly with all the commercialism and cultural festivities that surround this time of year. But we do well to help our children realize that Advent is a time of preparation, waiting, and hoping. It is different from Christmas. Various activities can reinforce this theme of waiting.

ADVENT CANDLES

Using an Advent wreath to mark this season before Christmas is a tradition among many churches and families. An Advent wreath is composed of five candles. Four candles placed in a circle are used for the four Sundays before Christmas. This circle of candles often in a wreath of evergreen represents the eternity of God. A center white Christ candle is lit on Christmas Eve and Christmas Day. The four Advent candles can be composed of a couple of combinations. Four purple or blue candles can be reminders of the church color of this season. One of the candles can be pink; it is called the Gaudete candle (gaudete is a Latin word meaning "rejoice"). It is used on the fourth Sunday in Advent to represent Christ's imminent arrival in the world.

A NATIVITY SCENE

Saint Francis of Assisi is credited with the first use of a crèche, or nativity scene. Using townspeople and animals, he staged a living nativity to teach the story of the birth of Jesus. Various crèches are available in stores. If there are young children in the home, be sure to get a nativity set that they can play with safely.

Put up the nativity scene on the first Sunday in Advent, or set it up gradually over the four Advent Sundays. Place the infant Jesus in the manger on Christmas Eve or Christmas Day. Since the arrival of the Magi is not celebrated until Epiphany (January 6), these figures can be added to the crèche at that time. Consider placing the Magi far from the crèche. During Advent and Christmas, move them closer to the crèche until they "arrive" on January 6.

ADVENT CALENDARS

Advent calendars have doors on them for each day in December beginning with December 1 through December 25. Behind each door is a Bible verse or scene leading up to the birth of Jesus. Young children in particular like this kind of physical counting down. Religious book and supply stores may be the best places to find an Advent calendar.

JESSE TREE

"A shoot shall come out from the stump of Jesse" (Isa. 11:1). From this scripture comes a tradition of recounting the spiritual heritage of Jesus. A Jesse tree is a branch of a tree (or a banner) hung with symbols that depict the salvation history of the Bible, beginning with creation and leading to the birth of Christ. Such a tradition reminds us that the birth of Jesus is part of God's grand design for humanity. Each day during Advent a new symbol is put on this tree. Check the library or a bookstore for books that provide patterns and directions for making a Jesse tree.

ADVENT BIBLE STORIES

The stories of Elizabeth and Zechariah, Mary, Mary and Elizabeth, Joseph, and the birth of John the Baptist can be read during Advent. Telling these stories during Advent is an important way of recognizing that Advent is a separate season from Christmas and has its own power and significance.

ADVENT AND CHRISTMAS HYMNS FOR MEALTIME PRAYERS

At mealtimes, sing a verse of an Advent or Christmas carol as your grace each day. Encourage different members of your family to choose songs they would like for the family to sing. This is also a good way to teach the great treasury of Advent and Christmas hymns.

CHRISTKIND AND PREPARING THE MANGER

For the German tradition of *Christkind,* or "Christchild," family members draw names at the beginning of the Advent season. Throughout the season each member does secret good deeds for the person whose name was drawn. The good deeds might include doing chores for someone, making baked goods or another small gift, writing notes, short stories, or poems, among other things. Together the family may want to brainstorm ideas before beginning this tradition. Young children in particular may need help with some ideas. On Christmas Eve or Christmas Day the Christkinds are revealed.

From construction paper cut out the shape of a manger. From yellow paper cut strips to represent straw. Place the manger in a prominent place where family members can readily see it. Each day at a specific time family members share the good deeds they have done for others that day. For every good deed a piece of "straw" is glued to the manger. By Christmas the manger will be filled with straw for the baby Jesus.

OTHER PREPARATIONS

Family, ethnic, and cultural traditions and activities can add richness to this season. Special celebrations during Advent such as Saint Nicholas Day and Saint Lucia Day can add to the meaning of this season. Activities such as baking, making and wrapping gifts, decorating homes, and attending special concerts and programs can celebrate this season. Personal reflection, scripture reading, and prayer are also important spiritual disciplines during Advent.

AN ADVENT PRAYER

God of hope and promise, as we enter this Advent season we ask that your calming presence be with us. Too often the promotions of our commercialized culture and family expectations make us feel overextended and anxious. Help us to focus on the journey ahead toward Bethlehem. Help us to find quiet moments in which to contemplate the purpose of this time of waiting. May your presence be felt in all of our preparations and planning. Give us ears to hear the alleluias of angels. Shepherd us toward the manger. Guide us like the Magi of old to find the Christchild. In the name of the One we await to be born to us. Amen.

• SAINT NICHOLAS DAY •

Saint Nicholas Day falls at the beginning of the Advent season (December 6). The origins of our modern Santa Claus have roots in the stories of this very real saint of the church. Saint Nicholas was a fourth-century bishop in Asia Minor (present-day Turkey). It is said that he had great love and compassion for children and poor people. Wearing the red robes of his office, he rode a white horse through town in the dark of night and left food and money for poor families. Often he flung the gold coins through the open windows of a house, and they fell into the shoes of those sleeping. After his death, people donned red clothes like the bishop's and anonymously left food, money, and gifts for people in need. Stories of Nicholas spread throughout Europe. Combined with other cultural traditions, the tradition of a gift-giving figure grew.

Exploring the roots of this holiday can be fun. Making Saint Nicholas spice cookies and giving them to neighbors and friends can be an enjoyable way to remember the stories of Saint Nicholas. Putting shoes or socks out on the eve of Saint Nick's day is a popular tradition. Small gifts, candy, and trinkets are placed in the stockings. Saint Nicholas can also leave food or money for the family to give to a local food pantry. Remembering lonely and homebound members of your community with a visit or homemade baked goods is another good way to celebrate this tradition.

A SAINT NICHOLAS CELEBRATION

Ahead of time, purchase small gifts that reflect the story of Saint Nicholas or might be used during the Advent or Christmas season. Items may include chocolate gold coins, small spice cookies, candy canes, nuts, socks, candles, or Christmas ornaments.

Gather a bag of nonperishable food items or several items for each family member. Another possibility is to have gift certificates indicating that a monetary gift has been made in the name of the family, or for each family member, to a local mission.

On the eve of Saint Nicholas Day, December 5, encourage each family member to put a pair of shoes by a fireplace, window, or door. During the night fill the shoes with the candy and small gifts. Also leave the bag of food items, or put canned goods next to each pair of shoes. Leave a note from Nicholas asking the family to take the food to the nearest food pantry on his behalf.

A PRAYER FOR SAINT NICHOLAS DAY

Compassionate God, on this feast day of Saint Nicholas, make us mindful of the example of discipleship this ancient brother of faith reflected in his life. In Christlike ways he cared for the poor and hungry, especially the children. In mysterious gift giving he has shown us the joy of servanthood. In our celebration this day, make us mindful that in reaching out to others, we truly reflect the hope of this Advent season. May we be more like Nicholas and share the abundance of our lives with others. In the name of the One who is coming, Emmanuel, we pray. Amen.

A BLESSING FOR SAINT NICHOLAS DAY

Holy Giver of all gifts, come and join us this day in our feasting and joy. As we delight in the mystery and gaiety of this Saint Nicholas Day, we ask your blessing. Bless especially the children. May their exuberance, playfulness, and dreams infect our lives. Bless our gift giving and receiving. May both reflect our sincerity and graciousness. Bless people in need of our compassion and care. May your presence be known to them through our acts of generosity. In the name of the holy child whose birth we wait and prepare for. Amen.

• SAINT LUCIA DAY •

Saint Lucia Day is celebrated in Sweden and other northern European countries. The legend tells of a young girl named Lucia who lived in Sicily around the year 300. She was executed by the Romans because of her Christian faith. Vikings invading Sicily heard of her story and took it back to the Scandinavian countries. Lucia was said to have been martyred on her birthday, December 13. This is the middle of the almost sunless winter months for northern European countries. But it is also close to the winter solstice. The winter solstice provided an opportunity for Scandinavian people to celebrate the return of the sunlight. Lucia's name means light. Her story and her name came to symbolize the coming of the light of Christ into the world.

Tradition says that the oldest girl in the family arises before sunrise on Saint Lucia Day. She puts on a white gown with a red sash (white for purity and celebration, red for the blood of a martyr). Her head is fitted with a wreath of green leaves and lit candles. She wakes everyone in the family by bringing special sweet rolls and coffee. During the Advent season, this old ritual can still remind us of the coming light of Christ into our world. It echoes the scriptures of Isaiah 9:2 and John 1:1–5.

Consider ways of adapting this tradition in your home on December 13. Make or purchase sweet rolls or coffee cakes for a special breakfast. Saint Lucia's Crown is such a breakfast treat. The recipe contains saffron to give the dough a yellowish color, again pointing toward light. Candles are put in the circle of braided dough and lit prior to eating. Candles can be lit on a morning breakfast table to greet family members as they awaken. Older children can help with special morning preparations and can awaken others to come to a special breakfast. Playing music or singing an Advent song is another way to awaken the household and greet this day.

A MORNING SAINT LUCIA CELEBRATION

The night before Saint Lucia Day, prepare a special breakfast table. Consider having an older child help with the preparations. Gather several candles and arrange them on a table or breakfast counter. If possible, arrange evergreens, holly, or other greenery around the candles. Purchase or prepare sweet rolls, morning buns, or coffee cake to serve at breakfast. Consider serving hot chocolate, special tea, or coffee. Set out the place settings needed for breakfast.

Early on the morning of December 13 awaken while it is still dark. Awaken family members, and have them gather at the breakfast table.(Or consider having the oldest child in a home awaken all the other members. The child can carry a candle or small flashlight as he or she gently wakes family members.) Light the candles on the breakfast table so that they are burning as family members arrive for breakfast (leave other lights off so that only the candles provide light). When all are gathered, begin the liturgy before eating.

Reader: Happy Saint Lucia Day! Today reminds us that the celebration of the birth of Jesus is very near. The birth of Jesus signals the coming of the light of God to the world.

Reader: Hear these words from Scripture. *(Read Isaiah 9:2 or John 1:1–5.)*

Reader: Let us hold hands this morning and pray:
Giver of hope and light, we welcome this Saint Lucia Day with joy! The lights at this table remind us of the light of Christ. Soon we will celebrate the birth of that Light into our world. Help us to remember that even in our gloomy times, the light of God shines through. May the warmth of this gathering, the sweetness of this meal, and the glow of these candles be with us all through this day. Amen.

Sing: Sing a stanza from an Advent song such as "O Come, O Come, Emmanuel."

As people are eating breakfast, share the story and tradition behind the celebration of Saint Lucia Day.

ADVENT CANDLE LITURGY 1

FIRST SUNDAY OF ADVENT

Reader: Today is the first Sunday of Advent. "Advent" means "coming." We are waiting and preparing for the coming of Christ. Let us light our first Advent candle, the candle of waiting.

(Light the first Advent candle.)

Reader: Hear these words from the prophet Isaiah. He was an ancient prophet, a spokesperson for God. This is what Isaiah said about the kind of Savior that God would send.

Reader: *(Read Isaiah 11:1–9.)*

Sing: "O Come, O Come, Emmanuel" (first verse).

Pray: **God of history, here we are at the beginning of Advent. Once again we await and prepare for the coming of your Christ. Guide us in our waiting. Help us to prepare our hearts and homes for the birth of the Bringer of Peace. Amen.**

SECOND SUNDAY OF ADVENT

Reader: As we relight our first Advent candle, let us remember that this is the season of waiting.

(Light the first Advent candle.)

Reader: Today is the second Sunday of Advent. We light our second candle to remind us that this is the season of hope. We wait and hope for the coming of the Messiah.

(Light the second Advent candle.)

Reader: Hear these words from Isaiah about the hope God gives us for a new way of living.

Reader: *(Read Isaiah 65:17–25.)*

Sing: "O Come, O Come, Emmanuel" (second verse).

Pray: **O God of all hope, we put our trust in you. As we look around in our world, we sometimes lose hope. In this season of preparation give us renewed hope. Remind us that the One who comes in your name comes to give us wholeness and new life. Come, Christ Jesus, quickly come. Amen.**

THIRD SUNDAY OF ADVENT

Reader: Let us relight the first two Advent candles, the candles that remind us this is the season of waiting and hoping.

(Light the first two candles.)

Reader: Today we light the third candle, the candle of joy. It reminds us of the joy that we will soon have at the coming of the Christchild.

(Light the third candle.)

Reader: Hear these words of joy from Isaiah. *(Read Isaiah 55:12–13.)*

Sing: "O Come, O Come, Emmanuel" (third verse).

Reader: Let us pray:
            O God, as we get nearer to the celebration of the birth of Jesus we are filled with joy and gladness. We know that your promises are true. We know that soon the waiting shall be over. Come into our hearts and make us ever mindful of the joy of this season. Amen.

FOURTH SUNDAY OF ADVENT

Reader: Today is the last Sunday of Advent. Let us light the first three Advent candles and recall what they remind us of. The first candle reminds us of waiting. The second candle reminds us of hope. The third candle reminds us of joy.

(Light three candles.)

Reader: Today we light the fourth candle. This candle reminds us of peace. As we wait and hope for the coming of God among us, we remember that Christ brings peace.

(Light the fourth candle.)

Reader: Hear how the prophet Isaiah describes the Messiah. *(Read Isaiah 9:6–7.)*
Sing: "O Come, O Come, Emmanuel" (fourth verse).
Pray: **O God, as this season draws to a close, we grow anxious with excitement at the coming of Christmas. Help us to remember in the days ahead that we wait for the coming of the Bringer of Peace in hope and joy. Teach us how to truly prepare ourselves and our world for the coming of this righteous Ruler. Amen.**

CHRISTMAS EVE OR CHRISTMAS DAY

Reader: Let us light the Advent candles one more time. They remind us that Advent is a season of waiting, of hoping, of joy, and of peace.

(Light the four Advent candles.)

Reader: Tonight *(or today),* our waiting is over. The child, the Chosen One of God, is born! Jesus comes to us as the Light of the world. Let us light the Christ candle to remind that Jesus is indeed the center of our lives and the Light to all the world.

(Light the Christ candle.)

Reader: Hear these words from the Gospel of John. *(Read John 1:1–5, 14–17.)*
Sing: "Joy to the World" (first verse).

Pray: **Gracious God, we give thanks that you have led us through the season of Advent to this day of celebration. We give thanks for the gift of Jesus. Help us to let the light of Jesus shine through us in the coming season of Christmas and throughout our lives. We pray in the name of the baby born in Bethlehem. Amen.**

ADVENT CANDLE LITURGY 2

FIRST SUNDAY OF ADVENT

Reader: Jesus said, "I am the light of the world. Whoever follows me will never walk in shadows but will have the light of life" (John 8:12). Let us light the first candle of Advent.

(Light the first Advent candle.)

Participant: Why do we light one candle today?

Reader: This candle reminds us of the light of hope that the prophets in the Hebrew Scriptures looked for with great expectation. They waited for a Messiah who would bring peace and love to the world. Prophets are people who speak on behalf of God. "Messiah" means "anointed one" or "chosen one of God."

Reader: Listen to these words from the prophet Isaiah. *(Read Isaiah 9:2b.)* During this season of Advent, we wait like people in the shadows for the coming of a light. Jesus is that light.

Sing: "O Come, O Come, Emmanuel" (first verse).

Pray: **O God, our world is in shadow. We need the light of peace and love to shine in our world. Help us to prepare our lives and our homes to receive the One who said, "I am the light of the world." We pray in the name of Jesus, our Savior. Amen.**

SECOND SUNDAY OF ADVENT

Reader: Jesus said, "I am the light of the world. Whoever follows me will never walk in shadows but will have the light of life."

(Light two candles.)

Participant: Why do we light two candles today?

Reader: The first candle reminds us of the light of hope for the prophets of old. The second candle reminds us of the gloomy night when Jesus and Mary found light and warmth in a stable. Here the Light of the world was born.

Reader: *(Read Luke 2:1–7.)* We are waiting for the light of that stable to shine once again.

Sing: "O Little Town of Bethlehem" (first verse).

Pray: **Gracious God, help us to have room in our hearts and our homes for other persons who need us. We thank you for friends and strangers who have received us when we were lonely or afraid or tired. May we be ready to receive the love God offers us in Jesus. We pray in the name of Christ, our Savior. Amen.**

THIRD SUNDAY OF ADVENT

Reader: Jesus said, "I am the light of the world. Whoever follows me will never walk in shadows but will have the light of life."

(Light three candles.)

Participant: Why do we light three candles today?

Reader: The first candle is a reminder of the light of hope of the ancient prophets. The second candle is a symbol of the light and warmth Joseph and Mary found in the stable. The third candle reminds us of the great light and joy that surrounded the shepherds at the announcement of the Savior's birth.

Reader: *(Read Luke 2:8–20.)* Like the shepherds, we rejoice that the birth of the Savior is near!

Sing: "The First Noel" (first verse).

Pray: **God of light and hope, as the humble shepherds went with rejoicing to the manger, may we come to Christmas with great joy and anticipation. Help us to share our joy and excitement with others in meaningful ways. We pray in the name of Christ, our Savior. Amen.**

FOURTH SUNDAY OF ADVENT

Reader: Jesus said, "I am the light of the world. Whoever follows me will never walk in shadows but will have the light of life."

(Light four candles.)

Participant: Why do we light four candles today?

Reader: The first candle reminds us of the light of hope of the ancient prophets. The second candle reminds us of the light and warmth of the stable. The third candle reminds us of the great light and joy that the shepherds experienced at the announcement of Jesus' birth. This fourth candle reminds us of the light of the star that guided the Magi to the Christchild.

Reader: *(Read Matthew 1:18–2:12.)* Like the wise and courageous Magi, we follow the light of a star to find the Light of the world.

Sing: "We Three Kings" (first verse).

Pray: **God of ancient prophets, new parents, humble shepherds, and wise Magi, lead us to your light. Keep us ever mindful of what our journey to Christmas is about. Help us to find the Light of the world in our hearts and in the faces of others. In the name of Christ, our Savior, we pray. Amen.**

CHRISTMAS EVE OR CHRISTMAS DAY

Reader: Jesus said, "I am the light of the world. Whoever follows me will never walk in shadows but will have the light of life."

(Light the four Advent candles and the center Christ candle.)

Participant: Why do we light this white candle?

Reader: We have waited for four Sundays for the coming of the Light of the world. That Light has finally come! We rejoice and celebrate the birth of God among us. We celebrate the birth of our Savior among us, the one who has come to light our way in this world.

Reader: *(Read John 1:1–5, 10–13.)*

Sing: "O Come, All You Faithful" (first verse).

Pray: **God of all hope and light, you have guided us to this day of celebration. Bless us that we might fully realize the power of this night *(day)*. Center our thoughts on the tiny babe whose birth among us we celebrate. Let us remember that this tiny one is the one chosen to bring your light into the world. Help us to let that light shine in all we do. In the name of Christ, our Savior, the Light of the world, we pray. Amen.**

• LAS POSADAS •

In Mexico, children celebrate the Christmas season from December 16 until January 6. On December 16 begins the nine-day celebration of Las Posadas. *Posada,* a Spanish word for "inn" or "lodging house," reminds the celebrants of the inn of Bethlehem.

There are two ways to celebrate Las Posadas. In the first, nine families collaborate, and each night the pilgrims, or *peregrinos,* go to a different house, looking for lodging. Each of the first eight nights they are denied admittance, but on the ninth night, Christmas Eve, they are welcomed into the house with much festivity.

The second way of celebrating is in one household, as family members process from door to door within the home, each time being turned away. Two small children carry images of Mary and Joseph who are looking for a place to stay where Mary can give birth to Jesus. Mary and Joseph move through the house symbolically, ever closer to that holy night. When on the ninth night they are admitted, they enter a room where the Nativity has been set up. Here they place the Christchild in the manger on Christmas Eve. A celebration with a piñata, songs, dance, and merriment follows until it is time to attend Christmas Eve church services. Consider inviting family members, neighbors, and friends to join you in having your own celebration.

Here is a Posadas meditation to use in your home. Each day provides an opportunity to act or reflect on the radical hospitality, the awesome mystery, the preparation, and the possibilities of the countdown until Christmas.

DAY ONE: LIGHT A CANDLE AND SAY A PRAYER FOR THE HOMELESS.

For example, pray:

Dear God, make us generous toward those who, like Mary and Joseph, are turned away and not given shelter. Transform our world into a welcome inn where the stranger, the refugee, and the displaced can find a warm place to sleep. We pray in the name of Christ, who came to us as an outcast and taught us how to welcome others. Amen.

DAY TWO: PRACTICE HOSPITALITY.

Set a beautiful table, even if you are ordering pizza. Set an empty place for the coming One who reminds us to be mindful of all who have no feast this day. Have the children make a special place card for each person, using a symbol of that person's particular gifts to decorate the card.

DAY THREE: PRACTICE GENEROSITY.

Reflect on the words of Saint Basil: "The bread which you do not use is the bread of the hungry; the garment hanging in your wardrobe is the garment of the one who is naked; the shoes you do not wear are the shoes of the one who is barefoot; the money that you keep locked away is the money of the poor; the acts of charity that you do not perform are so many injustices that you commit." Find that food donation barrel or clothing drop box—the opportunities will find you!

DAY FOUR: CLEAN UP AS A SPIRITUAL DISCIPLINE.

Clean out a junk drawer, the craft cupboard, the silverware container, or the mitten basket. Practice taking deep cleansing breaths as you clear out the clutter. Meditate on this opportunity to clean out the cobwebs inside you as well.

DAY FIVE: READ A PSALM OF PREPARATION.

Spend a few moments paging through the Psalms until you find one that speaks to you in the midst of your preparations. Reflect on a phrase or verse during the day. Write it on a note card, and put it above the kitchen sink. Put the verse on a sticky note, and affix it to the dashboard of the car. Use it as your table grace for the evening meal. Practice writing it in calligraphy. Try to memorize it. Send it in a Christmas card to someone unable to leave home. Use it as a breath prayer as you walk. Make the psalm your own.

DAY SIX: SANCTIFY YOUR ERRANDS.

Okay, errands must be done. So why not approach the shopkeepers, the dry cleaner, the checkout clerk, the librarian, and the florist as the saints of God? Remember the words of that great hymn, "I sing a song of the saints of God"? Think about these folks as the vast communion of saints, however harried or disgruntled they (or you) might be. Leave them with the blessing of patience, a smile, or a courteous word of thanks. It is a holy job, and somebody has to do it!

DAY SEVEN: MAKE A PIÑATA.

Blow up a balloon and cover it with papier-mâché. You may wish to embellish it with designs, cones, ears, or whatever that can be taped on and covered with papier-mâché as well. Let it dry. Pop the balloon. You will want to make a hole in the form to put goodies inside. When the outside is dry, paint it with two coats of tempera paint. Add doodads, sequins, ribbons, streamers, or glitter to make it as fancy as you would like. (In the interest of time, you can also purchase a piñata. But making one is more fun!)

DAY EIGHT: PRAY CRÈCHE PRAYERS.

Imagine all the people today who are making their way to the holy mangers of their lives: people on the threshold of dying, women going into labor, college students heading home, laborers punching the clock for a holiday reprieve, various shepherds and angels and peasants of today making their way home to the light. Keep them in your prayers of intercession.

DAY NINE: FIND TIME FOR SILENCE.

Silence is a great gift in this season of giving. Set aside five or ten minutes to sit in silence. Plop down in front of the illuminated Christmas tree, light the Advent candles, or try to come to church early and sit still in the pew before the Christmas Eve service. Breathe in the quiet. Center yourself in the center of the Christmas story, in the light and love that call to us from the manger. Pray for God's in-breaking Spirit to renew you in this season.

CHRISTMAS DAY: BREAK THE PIÑATA!

As the piñata bursts open, give thanks to God for the gracious outpouring of love this day, symbolized by the shower of goodies falling to the floor. Give yourself permission to do this activity, even if there are only adults at home or if you are the only one at home. The radical good news of the Christmas story should bring out the child in each of us. We all hunger for God's blessing and in-breaking presence. So celebrate with the spirit of a child, eager, even greedy for these great gifts!

—

A PRAYER FOR CHRISTMAS EVE

> O God, giver of every good gift, we stop and offer our
> thanks to you:
> for the gift of Jesus who fills us with song,
> for the gift of memory, which fills in the empty spaces,
> for the gift of witnesses like shepherds and innkeepers
> who carried the fire of the story and kept it alive,
> for the gift of parents and teachers who blew on the
> embers and kept the story alive in us,
> for twinkling lights and lingering aromas,
> for great expectations and silent waiting,
> for the aching we feel for the Day of Peace.
> O God of peace, give birth to joy and justice in each of
> us this night.
> Bless our gifts and our giving, in the name of your
> child, Jesus Christ. Amen.

Christmas

Yes, there are twelve days of Christmas! Christmas begins on December 25 and ends on January 5. Although much attention is given to the first day of Christmas, we do well to remember that this is a season of the church year. It celebrates the coming of God into the world in human form—the Word made flesh. "Emmanuel" means "God with us." The liturgical colors for Christmas are white and gold, signifying celebration. Consider ways to celebrate throughout the season.

Use the public library as well as family and friend connections to discover how other countries and cultures celebrate this season. Find out about English Boxing Day and the Feast of Stephen. Many traditions associated with Christmas originated from pagan rituals and myths. Early Christians adapted them to celebrate the birth of Jesus. Mistletoe, holly, ivy, evergreen, caroling, the wassail bowl, and holiday foods have interesting histories and adaptations. Learn about your cultural heritage for celebrating this season.

Take time each day to light a Christ candle as a visual reminder that the celebration of Christmas is truly Emmanuel, "God with us." Light the candle first thing in the morning or at a special time each day, such as a meal. When you have guests during the season, light the candle at the beginning of your festivities. The center of all celebration revolves around this presence of Christ who is born to us.

This season is rich in sacred and secular story and song. Read the fine literature that captures the meaningfulness of Christmas. *A Christmas Carol* by Charles Dickens, *The Best Christmas Pageant Ever* by Barbara Robinson, *How the Grinch Stole Christmas* by Dr. Seuss, "The Gift of the Magi" by O. Henry, the novella *The Other Wise Man* by Henry van Dyke, and the poem "Carol of the Brown King" by Langston Hughes are some literary treasures to be shared in your home during the season.

Sing Christmas carols throughout the holiday. Stores and radio stations stop the Christmas music on December 25. But during these twelve days, listen to Christmas music, go caroling with friends and neighbors, and teach the songs of the faith to children. Perhaps there are musicians in your family. They can play their instruments while others sing along.

Instead of unwrapping gifts all at one time, spread the gift giving over the entire twelve days. Save a gift for each day. Or have a family gift to open each day. Make gifts to give to others. Invite others to share in some of the gifts you have received. For instance, invite friends to listen to new music, play games, and share gifts of food and baked goods.

Go on family outings. There are often many concerts, movies, plays, and special programs offered during this holiday time. Take advantage of them with your family.

Consider giving the gift of yourself and time to others in need. Find out what mission opportunities are in your area. Helping out at a nursing home, prison, shelter, or other mission is a meaningful way to celebrate the love of God that is born to us.

At the end of the season think about having a Twelfth Night party. This tradition celebrates the end of the Christmas season. Music, feasting, and merrymaking were all part of this celebration. Funny gifts wrapped in white paper can be exchanged. Neighbors and friends can gather to have a bonfire of Christmas trees (if permitted in your community).

In all of your festivities, remember the cause for the celebration. Take time to reflect on the gifts this season offers to us. Take time to reflect on the gift God has given to us and its significance in our lives.

CHRISTMAS MORNING CELEBRATION
(Plan a simple Christmas breakfast such as sweet rolls, fruit, and juice. Put a candle in a special coffee cake or sweet roll.)

Sing: "Happy Birthday" to Jesus.

Pray: **Thank you, God, for this special day. We have waited so long for it. Be with us as we celebrate. In the midst of our fun, help us to remember the true gift of this season is the one you have given to us—Jesus the Christ. Help us to honor his birth by caring for others. Happy Birthday, Jesus! Grace us with your presence as we celebrate your coming to us. Amen.**

Liturgy for Christmas Day

After the flurry of morning unwrapping or breakfast preparations or church services or caroling, or into the silent still day, introduce this liturgy.

(Read the version of the Christmas story in Luke 2.)

Sing: A familiar carol.

Share: Encourage those gathered to play a musical instrument, recite a poem, or offer another gift.

A Prayer for the Twelve Days of Christmas
(Light a Christ candle before this prayer.)

Remind us, O God, that the party has just begun! Let us greet each day of this Christmas season as if it were the first. Let us keep the carols playing. Let us light the lights each day. Let the feasting continue. Let our hearts be filled with joy and excitement as in those first few hours of this Christmas. Help us to find ways to celebrate throughout these twelve days. In all our work and play this season, may we be like angels and shepherds telling the good news of Jesus' birth! Remind us that the joy of this birth lasts more than one day or even twelve. But each and every day of the year our lives celebrate the gift of Emmanuel—"God with us." Be with us in our joyful celebration in the days ahead. In the name of the babe born in Bethlehem we pray. Amen.

A Twelfth Night Celebration

Invite friends, family, or neighbors for a last day of Christmas party. Plan a special meal, or invite guests to bring a favorite food to share or Christmas leftovers.

Consider asking each guest or family to bring a small gift wrapped in white paper. It might be an ornament or other small symbol of the Christmas season. The gifts can be exchanged in a "grab bag" fashion during your party. (Another idea is to have people bring small gifts that will be given to a nursing home, shelter, or prison. Check with local agencies to see what kind of gifts might be appropriate.)

If any of your guests play musical instruments, invite them to bring them and share their music. If children will be present, consider having a piñata, treasure hunt, or surprise ball. (To make a surprise ball, take rolls of crepe paper and start to wind it into a ball. Every little bit tuck a small surprise or candy in the paper, and continue winding. This may take several rolls of crepe depending on the number of children. Have the children unwind the ball of paper little by little by rolling it to one another. The little treasures will be unwrapped as the ball is unwound.)

At the beginning of your celebration or before the meal, read the following liturgy.

(Light a Christ candle.)

Read: *(Read Isaiah 9:6–7, John 1:1–5, or other appropriate scripture.)*

Pray: **God of Emmanuel, we come to the close of this Christmas season with joy. We give you thanks for the gift of your love in the birth of Jesus. We give you thanks for the merrymaking that this season has given to us. As we gather one more time to celebrate, we ask that your holy presence dance among us. Bless our feast. Hear our music. Receive our laughter. Join our fun. At the end of this night, may we go forth proclaiming all the year through, "Glory to God in the highest and on earth peace." In the name of the One who is born to us in a stable. Amen.**

Sing: Have those gathered sing one or more favorite Christmas hymns.

• KWANZAA •

Kwanzaa, meaning "firstfruits," is a seven-day festival celebrated primarily by African Americans. It begins on December 26 and ends January 2. Kwanzaa is a time to recognize and celebrate the African heritage of African Americans. It is also a time to reflect on and celebrate the African American community in the United States. Swahili is the African language used to name many of the parts and symbols for Kwanzaa. There are seven principles of Kwanzaa. Each day of the festival celebrates one of these principles.

- First day—*Umoja* (Unity)
- Second day—*Kujichagulia* (Self-determination)
- Third day—*Ujima* (Collective work and responsibility)
- Fourth day—*Ujamaa* (Cooperative economics)
- Fifth day—*Nia* (Purpose)
- Sixth day—*Kuumba* (Creativity)
- Seventh day—*Imani* (Faith)

The central symbol is a candleholder, called a *Kinara,* which holds seven candles—three red, three green, and one black. Each day of Kwanzaa a candle is lit to reflect the number of the festival days. The color red reminds us of the blood African Americans have shed. Green is for hope and the color of Africa's land. Black is for the faces of the people.

Other symbols used for Kwanzaa include *Mazao* (fruits and vegetables), *Mkeka* (place mat), *Vibunzi* or *Muhindi* (ears of corn—one for each child in the home), and *Kikombe Cha Umoja* (community renewal cup).

Gifts are often given during Kwanzaa. They are to reflect the nature of the holiday and are most often handmade, or gifts of the self.

Kwanzaa does not replace Christmas. It can provide an opportunity not only to celebrate African American heritage but also to recognize God's presence in that heritage.

A BLESSING FOR KWANZAA

Holy One, we gather to celebrate our heritage and hope as your people. You have given us your "firstfruit" in the birth of Jesus. Help us to recognize and offer one another our firstfruits. May we give the fruits of unity, self-determination, community responsibility in work and wealth, a sense of purpose, our creativity, and our faith to better our homes, communities, and world.

Bless the children and elders, the youth and adults gathered here. May we learn from one another and recognize our strength together as your family. Bless those who do not gather with us. May they know of your love and know our love for them. Bless us with the gift of your empowering Spirit. We pray in the name of love incarnate, your wisdom and word made flesh among us, Jesus the Christ. Amen.

A TABLE LITURGY FOR THE FIRST DAY OF KWANZAA
(Have a Christ candle on the table along with the Kinara.)

Reader: Today we celebrate the beginning of Kwanzaa. We begin a special time of remembering and celebrating our ancestry, our life together now, and our hope for the future. We recognize the fruits of community and the interdependence we have upon one another. We light the Christ candle to remind us of our dependence upon Christ. Christ is the fruit of God. God has come to us and dwells with us in Christ.

(Light the Christ candle.)

Reader: *(Read one of the following: Psalm 98:1–9; Psalm 133:1–3; Psalm 145:1–21 [or parts of it]; Psalm 146:1–10.)*

Reader: We light the first candle on our Kinara. This is the candle of Unity.

(Light the first candle on the Kinara.)

Pray: **Holy Giver of life and hope, we gather during this Kwanzaa to remember where we have come from and what it means to live together as your people. Be with us in our celebration. As the Kinara candles are lighted each day, remind us that it is from you we are given gifts to achieve wholeness of life for ourselves and our community. We are your people, made in your image, a reflection of your presence in the world. Send your creative and empowering**

**Spirit to join us in our feasting. Come, Holy One, and
dance the dance of life and hope among us this Kwanzaa.
Amen.**

You may wish to create your own prayers as you continue to light the
Kinara candles and focus on each day's principle.

Epiphany

January 6 is the beginning of the Epiphany season in the church.
"Epiphany" means "manifestation" or "appearance." Epiphany celebrates
the coming of the Light of God into the world. The one who is born in a
stable in Bethlehem is the Savior of the whole world. The traditional
liturgical color for this season is white, symbolizing celebration and light.
Some church traditions use white for January 6, then green for the
remainder of the season until Lent.

According to tradition, January 6 is also the day when the church celebrates the arrival of the Magi. The story of the Magi's journey to find the
child Jesus is told to proclaim that even those in distant lands come to
recognize the importance of this event in human history. The wealthy
and the wise seek out this manifestation or incarnation of God made
flesh.

In the ancient church Epiphany was the original celebration of the
coming of Christ into the world. In Eastern Orthodox churches this is
still the case. In many parts of the world, such as Europe and Central and
South America, Epiphany, or Three Kings Day, is a more highly celebrated
day than Christmas. This is the day for gift giving, parties, and celebration in these cultures. In some countries children put their shoes out with
straw in them the night before Epiphany. The straw is for the Magi's
camels. The children hope in the morning to find that the straw has been
replaced with small gifts.

Rather than signal the end of Christmas, Epiphany is a festive and joyous celebration that can point us toward the future. Symbols such as crowns, stars, and candles can be used to decorate your home. Make paper crowns for everyone. Read the story of the Magi from Matthew 2:1–12, or read about the light of God coming into the world in John 1:1–5. Other stories and legends can add to the understanding of this season. Stories such as "The Ballad of Befana" by Phyllis McGinley, "Amahl and the Night Visitors," and "The Gift of the Magi" can be fun to read or tell.

Take this opportunity to make a Christ candle if you do not already have one or if you need a new one. Create mobiles of stars from construction paper, foil, and glitter, and hang them from a rod or coat hanger.

Invite friends and family to celebrate Epiphany. Prepare small gifts for everyone that depict the holiday. Make a Three Kings' Cake. Hide three pieces of candy and a nut in it. Those who find candy in their piece of cake get a paper crown and become Magi for the day. The one who gets the nut is designated Herod. The Epiphany party or Three Kings' Cake for next year is provided by this person. Have a piñata or crackers. (Crackers are party favors that pull apart with a "pop" to reveal small gifts and prizes inside.) Discover other ways to celebrate this season of light and hope in your home.

I. EPIPHANY CELEBRATION

On the eve of Epiphany, put a white cloth on the table. Encourage each member of the family to place a shoe on the table's edge. Put straw or excelsior in the shoes to provide symbolic food for the camels of the Magi. In the center, place the Christ candle. Overnight, place a star under the Christ candle at the center of the table, and connect the "beams" of the star to each shoe with yarn, gold ribbon, or crepe paper. Place a wrapped present in each shoe. Gifts could be gold jewelry, spices, massage oil, body lotions, herbs, teas, gold stars, star stamp with gold ink pad, or stickers. As the family members gather at the table, light the Christ candle.

Read: *(Read Matthew 2:1–12.)*

Sing: "We Three Kings" or "What Star Is This, with Beams So Bright."

Pray: **Thank you, God, for the gift of your Son, Jesus. We thank you for the light his life brings. We thank you for the gifts of each person in the family.**

(Name specific gifts such as the following:)

> For *(name's)* laughter,
> For *(name's)* cooking,
> For *(name's)* good ideas,
> For *(name's)* stories.
> We give you thanks. Amen.

II. EPIPHANY LITURGY
(Light the Christ candle.)

Read: *(Read Psalm 92:1–4.)*
Sing: Refrain of "We Three Kings."
Pray: **O Light of the world, we pray for all who sit in the shadows of sorrow or sadness. We pray for people who are lonely, for people who have lost loved ones, for people who are waiting through a long night of depression or despair. Bring your light to them. Let the Christ light shine in us that we might show forth your love to all. Amen.**

Gifts may be exchanged that symbolize light (candles, flashlights on key rings, stick-on stars that can be affixed to the ceiling and glow in the dark, prisms, origami paper for folding stars, etc.). Gifts may also be prepared for people in need (e.g., make little candle or star centerpieces for the meal trays that are delivered to Meals on Wheels, nursing homes, or the pediatric ward of the hospital).

III. EPIPHANY LITURGY
This liturgy is to be used after dark on January 6. It requires sparklers, candles, or light sticks for those present to hold and light. *(If possible, go outside to light the sparklers and candles and to sing the final song.)*

Reader: Let us hear the ancient words of the prophet Isaiah. *(Read Isaiah 60:1–3.)*

Reader: Let us remember this night the story of the Magi who journeyed to see the infant Jesus. *(Read Matthew 2:1–12.)*

Pray: **God of all grace and mercy, may the light of the sparklers (or candles) serve as a reminder of the heavenly star that guided the Magi to the Christchild. As you did for those ancient wise ones, help us to seek out the light of Christ in the world. In the year ahead, may we find ways in our lives to share the light and hope of Christmas every day, especially in times of sadness and despair. O Gracious Maker, make us reflectors of your divine light through Jesus Christ who is your Word made flesh—a light to the nations. Amen.**

(Light candles or sparklers.)

Sing: Gathered with candles or sparklers, sing "Joy to the World."

Reader: *(Read John 1:1–5.)* Let God's people gathered say, "Amen."

Reader: May the blessings of this night and this divine and life-giving light be ours in the journey ahead. Amen.

(If time permits, encourage those gathered to think about and discuss what it means to be a "light" for Christ in the world. Discuss specific examples.)

IV. AN EPIPHANY BLESSING

God of wonder and light, we celebrate the gift of Christ, the Light of the world. Bless us that we might be a reflection of that Light in all we do. As you did for the Magi of old, bless our pilgrimage of faith. May the stars in your heavens lead us always to the Christchild. May we find the presence of this Holy One in the faces of those in need of our wealth, wisdom, and love. Bless and guide all our work and play in the days to come. We ask it in the name of Jesus Christ, your Word made flesh, your Wisdom incarnate, your Light to the world. Amen.

Mardi Gras/Shrove Tuesday

The day before Lent begins is known as Mardi Gras, meaning "fat Tuesday." The first day of Lent is Ash Wednesday. In the early church the prelude to Lent was a time to use up the butter, fat, and meat in the house. During Lent these rich foods were not eaten. In some cultures, Mardi Gras is celebrated for several days before Lent begins. Mardi Gras is a time of carnival, costumes, and lavish parties. This excessive merrymaking stands in sharp contrast to the more austere and sacrificial season of Lent. Celebrating and feasting were not allowed in the early church. The absence of merrymaking was to remind people of the serious nature of the sacrifice Christ made on our behalf.

Shrove Tuesday is another name given to the Tuesday before Ash Wednesday. Often pancakes are served for the evening meal, because pancakes used up the last of the butter, eggs, and milk before the fasting of Lent began. Celebrating Shrove Tuesday or Mardi Gras can help us to prepare for the Lenten season. It is an experiential reminder of the excesses of our lives that tend to make us greedy and self-serving. Ash Wednesday, by contrast, launches us on a journey of sacrifice and servanthood.

For Shrove Tuesday plan a special meal and celebration in your home. You might want to invite friends and extended family to join your Mardi Gras party. Use balloons, streamers, and crepe paper to decorate your home. Set the table using festive colors, candles, a special centerpiece, and place settings. Party hats, noisemakers, and favors can also add to your celebration.

Consider having pancakes for the meal. Provide a variety of rich toppings such as fruits, nuts, chocolate chips, and whipped cream. Let everyone indulge this night in extravagant eating. Or instead of pancakes you may want to prepare a favorite family meal. Serve a rich dessert such as donuts, cheesecake, tarts, or ice-cream sundaes with all the fixings. If others are invited to your home, ask them to bring a favorite meal item or dessert.

Sing songs and listen to joy-filled music. Play group games during your celebration. Games such as charades and twenty questions are fun for people of all ages.

Dressing up in carnival costumes or masks is another way to add to this festive night. Using your creativity, make costumes or masks as simple or as extravagant as you wish with ordinary household items (e.g., paper bags, paper plates, egg cartons, pieces of clothing, pipe cleaners) or fancier items (e.g., glitter, feathers, sequins). Consider a theme in designing these creations: Bible characters, favorite storybook characters, someone or something you wish you could be, what you like or dislike. Making these masks or costumes can be done before your celebration or as part of the evening's festivities. Take time to look at and appreciate everyone's creation. Share what the mask or costume might represent to the person who made it.

In whatever way you choose to celebrate this night before Lent, begin and end with prayer.

The movement of the celebration should be from exuberant joy to quiet contemplation. Toward the end of the evening, talk about the coming season of Lent. For young children, you may need to be prepared with simple explanations.

PRAYERS FOR THE BEGINNING OF
A SHROVE TUESDAY CELEBRATION

Pray: **God of feasting, we gather this night to revel in the abundance and richness of life. Indulge us with your holy presence. May your Spirit dance and play among us this night. Bless all those gathered for this feast of food, fun, and companionship. We sing of your praise with all the faithful in heaven and on earth. Alleluia, alleluia, alleluia! Amen.**

           (Have those gathered repeat, "Alleluia, alleluia, alleluia! Amen.")

Sing: *(After the prayer those gathered may sing a song of praise and joy.)*

Pray: **God of festival and fun, God of joy and jubilation, bless us this night as we celebrate the joy of being your people. Thank you for this special meal that reminds us of all the richness life has to offer us. Thank you for the fun and laughter of this night. Join us, Holy One, and grace us with your playful presence. Amen.**

PRAYERS AT THE END OF A
SHROVE TUESDAY CELEBRATION

Read: *(Read Isaiah 58:6–7.)*

Pray: God of holiday and holy day, we give you thanks for the time of joy-filled celebration. As we enter Lent, remind us of the kind of fasting you truly desire from us. Help us to fast from selfish desires and needs. Help us to learn your way by following the way of Jesus. May your presence guide us in the days ahead until once again we will sing, Alleluia, alleluia, alleluia! Amen. (Have those gathered say to one another, "God be with you.")

– or –

God of feasting and fasting, we have come to the end of this night of merriment. Thank you for joining us in our fun. Now join us as we begin the season of Lent. Help us to fast from things that keep us from doing your will. Help us to feast on the joy of loving servanthood on behalf of Christ. In the name of our crucified and risen Savior. Amen.

Lent

Lent begins on Ash Wednesday. It lasts for forty days, not counting Sundays. (Sundays are not counted because they are considered "little Easters" or "resurrection days.") We prepare for the coming of our Sovereign through repentance.

Lent is a season of personal and corporate repentance, reflection, study, meditation, and prayer. It is a time to examine how we are living our lives as servants of Christ. It is also a time to recall the ministry, passion, and death of Jesus. In the ancient church it was a time to prepare converts for baptism into the church on Easter. The liturgical color for Lent is purple. Purple is a color signifying repentance as well as royalty. The color reminds us of our need for self-reflection and repentance, as well as reminds us of the royalty of Jesus Christ in his passion and death.

Ash Wednesday begins this season with a reminder of our humanity and the gift of Christ as our Savior. Ashes are a sign of humility and repentance. The word "repent" means to "turn around," to change our ways and become more in line with God's intentions for our lives.

Lent culminates with Holy Week. This week prior to Easter recounts the last events in the life of Jesus. It begins with Palm or Passion Sunday, which celebrates the triumphal entry of Jesus into Jerusalem. Maundy Thursday commemorates the Last Supper and Jesus' commandment, or mandate, that his disciples love one another as he loved them. The word "maundy" comes from "mandate." Good Friday is the day of Jesus' crucifixion. It was originally called God's Friday. Holy Saturday is the bridge between Good Friday and Easter Sunday. On this day we recall that Jesus lay in the tomb.

In the history of the church Lent has often been abused with excessive penance, token abstinence, or self-righteous satisfaction of self-denial. In modern times Lent has often been devoid of any meaning and ignored by Christians. But this season can serve as an important time to intentionally examine our discipleship and servanthood on behalf of Christ.

Engage in a mission project together during Lent. Consider ways in which your family can serve others on behalf of Christ. Perhaps others in your church would join your family in this mission.

Read an entire Gospel. Review the ministry of Jesus, and become more familiar with one of the Gospels. Beginning with the first chapter and verse of a Gospel, read scripture together each day during Lent. Discuss the meaning of the passage. What do the verses tell us about Jesus? What do they tell us about ourselves as followers of Jesus?

Begin the daily discipline of praying together if your family does not have a regular prayer time. You may want to pray during mealtime or before bed. Use a traditional prayer from your church or family history. Encourage people to voice their own prayers of thanks as well as concerns. Pray on behalf of others. These are called prayers of intercession.

Bring out symbols of Lent. Christian symbols remind us of our faith. If you have special symbols that remind you of Christ, the Lenten season, or the events of Holy Week, put them on your meal table or other prominent place in your home. Leave them out for the Lenten season. If you do not have any, make some (e.g., a cross, clay cup and loaf, a purple table runner, a banner).

• ASH WEDNESDAY •

Provide a simple family meal, such as soup and bread, but no dessert. The simplicity of your meal can provide an opportunity to discuss the meaning of the season of Lent. If you have celebrated Shrove Tuesday the day before, compare the differences in the meals. Talk about what it means to be servants of Christ and to sacrifice on behalf of others. Share ideas for ways that your family can observe Lent. If your church has provided lenten devotional materials, begin them today.

Place a pretzel at each place for your Ash Wednesday meal. In medieval times monks baked bread to provide an income. During Lent they baked pretzels (no fat, milk, or eggs are used). The monks used the shape of the pretzel to teach about prayer and the Trinity. The shape is a reminder of arms folded across the chest in penitential prayer. The three holes are reminders of God as made known to us as the Creator, the Savior, and the Holy Spirit. Each Wednesday of Lent prepare a simple meal and place a pretzel at each place as a reminder of prayer.

Ahead of time, prepare small pieces of paper with crosses on them for each member of your family. Take time to think about what kind of Lenten discipline each person may observe. Write or draw these on the paper. Encourage each person to keep the paper in a place that will be a reminder of this discipline.

Attend Ash Wednesday service at church. The Christian faith is a communal one. It is important that the community of faith joins together to enter into the season of Lent. Worship together as a family.

Use one of the following prayers on Ash Wednesday when your family is gathered together.

PRAYER BEFORE A MEAL

Gracious and loving God, may this simple meal remind us of the simplicity of Christ's life. Our lives often become cluttered with excesses that keep us from being your servants. Help us this Lent to follow more clearly the way of Jesus. Bless and guide our path ahead. In the name of our crucified and risen Savior. Amen.

PRAYER FOR GUIDANCE DURING LENT

(In preparation, family members need to think of a concrete behavior, attitude, or action they would ask God to help them change during Lent. Do not force anyone to voice a prayer that he or she wishes to pray silently.)
Loving God, as we begin this season of Lent, we ask that you help us become more faithful followers of Jesus. Hear us as we pray and ask for your help.

(Each person says:) God, please help me to _____.
(Everyone responds after each petition:) Hear our prayer, gracious God.

God, help us to truly repent and change our ways. Be with us in the weeks ahead. We ask in the name of our Savior, Jesus the Christ. Amen.

PRAYER FROM PSALM 51 (READ PSALM 51:1-2, 10-12, OR THE ENTIRE PSALM)

God of all mercy and steadfast love, we do not always live the way you want us to. Forgive us. Help us during this season of Lent to examine how we can be more faithful followers of Jesus the Christ. Guide our journey of discipleship. May our words and deeds truly reflect your will. In the name of Jesus, our Savior, we pray. Amen.

• PALM SUNDAY •

If you receive palms from your church today, consider using them in your celebration. Weave three palms leaves into a crown. Fold one into a cross. Take the crowns, crosses, or palm branches to those who could not be in worship, to those who are ill or who cannot leave their homes. This will remind them of this special day.

PALM SUNDAY TABLE LITURGY

(Use palm branches as a table centerpiece. Lay them on the table and place a Christ candle in the center. Light the candle at the beginning of the meal.)

Read: *(Read Psalm 24:7–10.)*

Pray: O mighty God, our strength and our help, today we remember the coming of Jesus into Jerusalem. Our hearts shout and sing joyful praises to your name. Hosanna, blessed be the One who comes in your name! Holy Jesus, come into our lives today. Go before us and lead the way. Grant us the courage to follow. Amen.

PALM SUNDAY BLESSING

Triumphant God, today we wave palm branches and sing loud hosannas to honor the One who comes in your name. Bless these branches that they may serve as a reminder of your majesty and our praise. We are mindful that today marks the beginning of a week of sorrow and pain. Bless us as we leave the palms behind and begin our journey toward the cross. May our joy this day and our hope in you sustain us in the days of suffering ahead. In the name of Jesus Christ, our crucified and risen Savior. Amen.

• HOLY WEEK •

Find time each day to read from the Scriptures about the last events in the life of Jesus. You may choose to read before or after a family meal, or you may set aside a special time each day to read them together.

Here is a sample reading list. Choose *one* of the readings suggested for each day. Consider a symbol to use each day to remind you of the event in the passage. After you read the daily scripture, place your symbol in the center of your meal table or another prominent place in your home. By the end of the week you will have collected visual reminders of these events.

- Palm Sunday—Matthew 21:1–9; Mark 11:1–11; Luke 18:35–43
- Monday—Matthew 21:18–19; Mark 11:15–19; Luke 19:45–48; John 2:13–17
- Tuesday—Matthew 26:6–13; Mark 14:3–9; Luke 7:36–50; John 12:1–8
- Wednesday—Matthew 26:1–4; Mark 14:1–2; Luke 22:1–2; John 11:47–53
- Maundy Thursday—Matthew 26:14–75; Mark 14; Luke 22; John 13:1–20; 18:1–27
- Good Friday—Matthew 27; Mark 15:1–41; Luke 23:1–49; John 18:27–19:37
- Holy Saturday—Matthew 27:57–61; Mark 15:42–47; Luke 23:50–56; John 19:38–42

Attend the special worship services that your church offers this week. Most churches have services for Maundy Thursday and Good Friday. Plan on attending them with your family. Some communities have ecumenical services during the week. They are a good way to witness to the wholeness of the Christian church. Times and places of quiet prayer and meditation are offered on Good Friday and Holy Saturday in some churches. Take time out from your schedule to go and sit quietly and reflect on the power of these events.

• MAUNDY THURSDAY AND GOOD FRIDAY •

Many churches have special services of communion and Tenebrae on Maundy Thursday. Sometimes a meal may precede the worship service or be part of the liturgy. Attend worship as a family in your community of faith.

Some communities have an ecumenical Good Friday worship. It is a strong reminder that despite differences in traditions, the Good Friday event is central to all Christians. Services are held at noon, between noon and three o'clock, or in the evening. Some churches open their sanctuaries for quiet prayer and reflection sometime throughout the day. Fasting from solid food is still a discipline that many Christians follow to help in remembering the pain of this day. Although fasting is not advised for small children, some sacrifice of food can be a concrete way of observing this day.

Do not be afraid to include children in worship or other observances of Maundy Thursday and Good Friday. Even very young children can appreciate the quiet, somber, and reflective nature of these days. It is important that they begin to develop a sense of the tragedy of these last days of Jesus' life. When they do so, the miracle of Easter becomes even more glorious to them.

A MAUNDY THURSDAY TABLE LITURGY

This liturgy is not intended to supplant a communal experience in the congregation. This celebration may take place before going to an evening worship service or may set the theme for the family to attend a service on Good Friday.

You will need place cards with names of the people at the Last Supper (you will find the names of the disciples in Luke 6:13–16; you may also wish to include a few background people, such as a servant, a cook, the host's family); a loaf of bread (preferably homemade—plan a bread-baking project as a family); a pitcher of grape juice; your regular meal (perhaps a favorite of the kids, such as macaroni and cheese); a Bible; a Christ candle; and a hymnal. (Note here anything else you may want to include: _____.)

Set the table, putting the disciple place cards at each family member's customary place at the table. Or just circle the place cards around the table to represent the symbolic presence of the twelve disciples around Jesus at the center as represented by the loaf and the cup. As people sit down to the meal, light the Christ candle, and invite them to imagine that they are the people on the place cards—Jesus, Judas, Peter, or one of the characters not mentioned but probably present. You may want to carry on the entire dinner conversation as if you were those characters, or just initiate a brief discussion about what that person's experience of the Last Supper might have been. Tailor the conversation to the ages, knowledge, and tolerance (!) of those gathered.

Following the meal, continue the liturgy with these suggestions:

Sing: Sing the Dakota Indian hymn "Many and Great, O God, Are Thy Gifts" (hymn 3 in *The New Century Hymnal;* also in other denominational songbooks), and ask one of the family members to provide a steady drumbeat. Or pick the Doxology or another song that is well known in the family circle.

Read: *(Read Luke 22:14–23.)*

Pray: *(Blessing of the bread:)*
          Bless this bread, O God. Like all our gifts, it comes from you. We have merely added our kneading and patting and waiting and cooking and cooling. We thank you for this time together to taste and savor your presence.
          (Blessing of the cup:)
          We are thirsty, God. Thirsty for peace in the world and inner peace. Thirsty for meaning. Thirsty for you. Bless this cup as we are refreshed. Help us to remember Jesus and his life and ministry.

All break off a chunk of bread (be generous with God's gifts!) and all drink the juice. Allow for talking, laughing, a natural, normal exchange—not a formal, somber time. When all have eaten and finished the juice, conclude the evening meal with this prayer or one like it:

Be with us this night, O God. Walk with us through our valley of the shadow of death. Stay with us in our Garden of Gethsemane. Give us courage to face the Good Friday of our own faith, even as we remember the sacrifice of Jesus. Help us to stand up for our faith in difficult times, and to shoulder the consequences of discipleship. Amen.

PRAYER FOR MAUNDY THURSDAY

Gracious and loving God, we remember this is a holy night. We remember that Jesus gathered with his disciples to eat his last meal. We remember that he gave a new commandment to serve and love others. We remember that he blessed wine and bread. We remember that he prayed to you for strength. We remember that he was betrayed with a kiss. Let us also remember that these events of so long ago are part of us. Forgive us if we do not realize our own participation in these events. For it is we who sit at the table and hear the commandment of Jesus. It is we who fall asleep and continue to betray our Savior. Help us to follow the way of Jesus the Christ. Grant us your blessing this night. Amen.

GOOD FRIDAY LITURGY

Read: Today we remember that Jesus died. It is a day of sadness. Hear these words from Scripture.

Read: *(Read one of the following: Psalm 22:1–2; 130; Isaiah 50:4–8; 53:1–6 or 1–12; or one of the Gospel accounts of Good Friday.)*

Read: Even though this is a sad day, we have hope. We know that today is not the end. We wait for God's saving power to come. We put our trust and faith in God. God will not disappoint us.

Pray: **God of hope and deliverance, we wait in the gloominess of Good Friday. All creation mourns this day. We cry for the cruel death of your Child. We cry because the world is still filled with such pain and brokenness. Forgive us for adding to that pain and brokenness. Accept our tears this day. May our grief turn soon to gladness. Amen.**

• HOLY SATURDAY •

Holy Saturday is a quiet and anticipatory day in the life of the church. It is a time to prepare for Easter. Involve children in your preparations. (See the section on Easter.) Some congregations hold prayer vigils during the day or evening. Church sanctuaries are open for prayer and meditation.

The great Easter vigil is an ancient service that awaits the dawn of Easter. At this service converts were baptized into the Christian faith. This service is traditionally held around midnight and into the early hours of Easter morning. Some congregations continue this tradition or a variation of it. It is a highly symbolic, dramatic, and beautiful service. It contains four major aspects: scripture readings of God's redeeming work in Christ, light, water, and communion.

HOLY SATURDAY PRAYER

God of tomb and stillness, be with us this day in our waiting. We wait with anticipation the passing of your Child from death to life. In this passover we await our own renewal into life with Christ. Be with us this day in our preparations for the glorious day of resurrection. Prepare our hearts, minds, and souls as we prepare our homes and outer selves. In the name of the crucified and soon to be resurrected one, Jesus the Christ. Amen.

Easter

Easter is the height of the church year. We celebrate the decisive event in our faith history: God's victory over death—the resurrection of Jesus Christ! The resurrection announces that the future of God has already begun. It is a time of exuberant rejoicing. The great fifty days of Eastertide begin on Easter Sunday and last until Pentecost. Compared to the stark and somber time of Lent, Easter is unfettered joy and triumph of God's power and ultimate authority over all life. In the early church Easter Sunday was the traditional time for new converts to be baptized. Many churches today include celebrations and renewal of baptismal vows in Easter morning worship. The liturgical colors for Easter are white and gold for celebration.

The word "Easter" comes from "oster" or "Easter," a name for the pagan goddess of spring, or dawn in northern Europe and the British Isles. Early Christians adopted this word and transformed its meaning. Easter signals the continual rebirth and new beginnings that God offers us through Christ. The celebration of the resurrection of Christ is the event that initiated the beginning of the dominion of God.

As with many of our Christian celebrations, Easter is a blending of pagan, ethnic, and religious symbols and practices. These can be combined in our homes to provide meaningful expressions of faith. Involve all members of the household in your Easter preparations.

Attend Easter worship services with family and friends. If your family is up early, consider attending a sunrise service. If you are traveling over Easter Sunday, find a church to attend and enjoy another faith community's celebration.

Create an Easter tree. Several weeks before Easter cut a branch from a bush or tree that will bud within a few weeks. (Willow tree branches and forsythia bushes are two good examples.)

Put the cut branch into a clay flowerpot filled with small rocks, sand, or dirt. Keep the filler moist. By Holy Saturday the cutting should have rooted and begun to have small leaves or buds growing. On Holy Saturday or early on Easter Sunday, hang small symbols on your tree cutting that symbolize the Christian faith, or new life. You can buy or make these symbols. Hang objects such as eggs, crosses, doves, a rainbow, butterflies, lambs or flowers. Keep your Easter tree up throughout the fifty days of Eastertide.

Bake Easter bread. Bread is a powerful reminder of our new life in Christ. Several ethnic and cultural traditions serve a special bread on Easter Sunday. Consider making and serving a bread at one of your family meals on Easter Sunday. Find out if there is a particular kind of Easter bread served in your family's ethnic background or history. Look through recipe books to find a bread recipe to use.

If you do not want to make the bread from scratch, buy frozen bread dough. Follow the directions for thawing the dough. Shape the dough into a three-braided twist, cross, butterfly, or other Easter symbol. Bake as directed and serve on Easter.

Decorate eggs. Eggs have long been a symbol of rebirth and new life. The tradition of decorating and coloring hard-boiled eggs goes back to pre-Christian times. This is a fun activity for family members of all ages. Use commercial egg dyes for this project, or consider making your own egg dyes from natural ingredients in your home. With crayons write words or draw symbols that celebrate Easter on the eggs before they are colored. Use words and symbols such as "Alleluia," "Christ is risen," crosses, butterflies, Chi-Rho, or Alpha and Omega.

Make a Christ candle on Holy Saturday. If you do not have a Christ candle for your home, Easter is a good time to begin using one. (See the directions for making a Christ candle earlier in the book.)

Set out remembrances of family baptisms: baptism candles, certificates, pictures, or other mementos. Easter is a time for remembering and renewing our baptismal vows. Light the baptismal candles. Look at the pictures. Tell stories of each member's baptism.

Reach out and share the good news of Easter with others. Invite neighbors, friends, coworkers, or others to share an Easter meal with your family. Give small gifts or tokens of the season to those who are lonely or unable to leave their homes. Gifts such as flowers, seed packets, children's drawings of Easter, baked goods, or candles can be given to others in celebration of Easter.

Give a gift to a local or church mission from your family in honor of Easter. It might be a gift of your family's time, talents, or treasures. You may choose to do this on Easter Sunday or at any time throughout the Easter season.

Plan a festive Easter meal. Set the meal table with a white tablecloth, table runner, or place mats with gold accents. Arrange a centerpiece. Use flowers or plants, colored eggs, a Christ candle, baptismal candles, or other candles. Make table favors for each person. At each table setting place one of the following: a colored Easter egg with "Alleluia" written on it, a shell with the person's name on it as a reminder of baptism, a small Easter cross, or some other appropriate sacred symbol for Easter.

BLESSING FOR EASTER BREAD

Source of all life, bless this bread. In its breaking, may we remember the last supper of Jesus and his disciples. In its sharing, may we recall we are part of your new creation. In its eating, may we have a taste of your future banquet, a feast where all people will sit together at your table. Like the tiny yeast within this loaf, may our faith grow and yield nourishment for the world. In the name of our bread of life, Jesus Christ, our risen Savior. Amen.

EASTER TABLE LITURGY

Reader: We welcome this feast of Easter, this feast of joy and renewal. Today we proclaim the good news of God's eternal love for us. Nothing can separate us from that love of God in Christ! As we light this candle, let us remember that the Word of God was made flesh in this world through Jesus the Christ. The Light shone in the shadows. And the shadows did not overcome it!

(Light the Christ candle.)

Reader: Let us remember that we are to reflect the light of the risen Christ in our lives. We are called as apostles to spread the good news of this day to all the world. Christ is risen! Alleluia!

(Light any other candles on the table.)

Reader: Let us pray.

Victorious God, we remember that it was in the breaking of bread that the disciples realized the presence of the risen Christ among them. Be present with us in our feasting and celebration. We give you thanks for all the blessings this Easter brings to us. We give you thanks for the hope and joy that your victory over death assures for us. We give you thanks for new life that springs around us, even when we do not perceive it. We give you thanks for the communion of saints who join us this day. Bless this table and those gathered around it. Bless and guide us throughout this Easter season that we might be able to realize the presence of the risen Christ in our midst. In the name of our risen Savior we pray. Amen.

Reader: Let all of us show our thanksgiving and praise to God by saying, "Thanks be to God. Alleluia. Amen!"

Response: Thanks be to God. Alleluia. Amen!

AN EASTERTIDE PRAYER

Renewing and re-creating God, we rejoice in this Easter season. All around us is evidence of your saving power. In the return of spring we witness the rebirth of life in plants and animals. Within our hearts seeds of hope are given new roots. Help us to become the new creations in Christ that you call us to be. Help us to be Easter people, people who live out the good news of the risen Christ. Amen.

PSALMS FOR EASTERTIDE

During the season of Easter, use one of the following psalms as your morning, evening, or meal prayer: Psalms 9, 11, 47, 98, 117, 136, 145, 150. Read all or part of the psalm. Or on each Sunday during the Easter season, light your Christ candle at a mealtime and read one of the psalms. There may be other psalms that you enjoy. Any psalm that sings of God's praise and saving grace is appropriate during Eastertide.

Pentecost

Pentecost celebrates the beginning of the Christian church. It marks the day when the followers of Jesus were filled with God's Spirit and began to preach the good news of Jesus Christ. The story in Acts 2:1–21 tells in a wonderfully poetic and dramatic way this birth of the church. Pentecost also reminds us that God's Spirit empowers all of us. Particularly in times when we feel that empowerment, God breathes new life into us. We are all called to share the Spirit of God that burns within us and proclaims the saving power of Christ.

In preparation for Pentecost, decorate your home with symbols of this feast day. The colors for Pentecost are red and white. Red is for the fire of the Spirit and martyrs of the faith. White is for celebration and the dove, symbol of the Holy Spirit. Doves, flames, wind socks, and kites can become decorations. Candles, special place cards, red napkins, or a red tablecloth can be used on a meal table. Children can help to make some of the decorations using various art media. Make mobiles of flames and doves. Make or decorate a family kite, and plan an outing to fly it. Wind socks can be made from material, ribbon, paper, or paper bags. Pinwheels can be bought or made and given to each person as a remembrance of the day.

If young children will be present, consider using a cake with candles to celebrate Pentecost as the birthday of the Christian church. Invite church members, neighbors, and friends to share a meal in your home. Have everyone bring a red food. Such a gathering can remind us of the diversity of the Christian church. Acting out the story of Pentecost in Acts or the dry bones story from Ezekiel 37:1–14 can be fun for people of all ages. Include songs that celebrate the presence, power, and spreading of God's Spirit such as "Every Time I Feel the Spirit," "Pass It On," or "Spirit of Gentleness."

PENTECOST PRAYER

(*Light a Christ candle. Ask persons gathered to hold hands.*)

God of wind and fire, God of spirit and flame, come into our gathering. As we feel one another's hands, may we feel the power of your presence. Set our hearts aglow and infuse us with your power that we might be

renewed to proclaim your Word. Join us in our celebration this day. And when we depart from one another, send us forth with your blessing, empowered once again to be your disciples. Amen.

LITANY FOR PENTECOST
(Instruct those gathered that the following prayer is a litany. After each petition, they are to respond with, "Come, Holy Spirit." After this instruction, you may light a candle.)

Reader:	Holy One, come and be present with us again this Pentecost.
Response:	Come, Holy Spirit.
Reader:	Send your mighty wind to break down the barriers that separate us from our brothers and sisters in this world.
Response:	Come, Holy Spirit.
	With tongues of fire, rekindle our hearts to glow with your presence.
Reader:	Come, Holy Spirit.
Response:	Remind us that we are part of your vision for humanity.
Reader:	Come, Holy Spirit.
Response:	Send your gentle and sustaining love to bind our hearts together as your people.
Reader:	Come, Holy Spirit.
Response:	In the name of Jesus the Christ. Amen.

A TABLE LITURGY FOR PENTECOST
(If possible, have different people, including children and elders, read.)

Read:	Today we gather to celebrate Pentecost. We remember the beginnings of the Christian church. We celebrate the presence of God's empowering Spirit among us today. We hope for the future visions and dreams of God's people to come to full fruition. We light three candles to remind us this day of our past, present, and future as God's people. We light three candles to remind us of God's revelation among us as Creator, Savior, and Holy Spirit.

(If possible, have three different individuals light the candles.)

Read: *(Read Psalm 104:1–4 or Acts 2:1-20.)*

Pray: God of living Spirit, who came to your people in ages past, come again. Join us in our feast this day. Rejoice with us as we celebrate the birthday of the Christian church. We give you thanks for the gift of Jesus Christ. We give you thanks for your steadfast presence in our lives. We give you thanks for the parade of disciples throughout history who have been empowered by your Spirit. May we at this table feel the rush of your mighty breath and the heat of your power within us. Bless our feast and all those gathered here, in the name of Jesus Christ. Amen.

A Prayer in Many Languages

(Invite others to share the Pentecost celebration in your home. Include guests who can speak various languages. Have those gathered participate in a prayer in one of the following ways: say a common prayer together, such as the Prayer of Jesus, inviting those who can speak in a different language to do so, or have the following prayer read in different languages.)

> God of holy wind and sacred fire,
> Today we celebrate the power and presence
> Of your Spirit among all humanity.
> Through Jesus Christ we are united as one body.
> May your visions and dreams of shalom,
> Proclaimed by your prophets,
> Be made a reality in our midst.
> Come, Holy One.
> Bless those gathered here in your name.
> Celebrate this day of renewal and hope with us.
> Breathe into us new life.
> Send us forth to be your witnesses
> To the ends of the earth and beyond. Amen.

Common Time

The season of the church year from Pentecost until Advent is called Common Time. It has also been referred to as Trinity Season and Ordinary Time. It is time in the church calendar that celebrates the growth of Christian discipleship. The traditional liturgical color for this season is green, symbolizing growth. In the ordinariness of our lives, in the common day-to-day routine of work and play, we are called to continually sink our roots deep into the soil of faith that we might bear fruits of God's Spirit. Although Common Time does not contain a major festival of the church year, it includes several important celebrations.

PRAYER FOR CHRISTIAN GROWTH

Gardener God, you have planted us in your world. You nourish us and nurture us. You have sent Christ to be our example and to sow seeds of faith. In this season of Christian growth help us to sink our roots deep into the soil of faith. May we grow in our knowledge and understanding. May the fruits of our faith be made evident by our actions. May we tend not only to our own faith, but also to the faith planted in others. Help us to spread seeds of discipleship. We ask in the name of Christ, our true vine. Amen.

• TRINITY SUNDAY •

Common Time begins on Trinity Sunday, the first Sunday after Pentecost. The mystery of God and human knowledge of God are always unfolding. Trinity Sunday celebrates our understanding of God in three primary ways:

1. We understand God as the Creator.
2. God comes to us in human form in Jesus the Christ.
3. God is ever present in our lives as Spirit.

Creator, Savior, and Spirit—this threefold description of God helps us to discern the nature of God and the ways in which God works in the world.

A TRINITY SUNDAY PRAYER
(Place three candles of equal size on a table.)

Read: God is a mystery. There are three ways that we have come to understand God. God is our Creator and the Creator of the world. *(Light one candle.)* God has come to humanity in human flesh as Jesus, the Christ. *(Light the second candle.)* God's power is ever present as Spirit. *(Light the third candle.)*

Pray: **Holy God, you are mysterious and powerful. You are made known to us as Creator, Christ, and Spirit. Help us to grow in our understanding of your character. Help us to be open to new understandings of who you are. May we seek to always honor you. Bless us, O Creator, with your compassionate love. Grant us through Christ your boundless grace. By your ever present Spirit guide and empower our lives that we may grow in discipleship. Amen.**

• REFORMATION SUNDAY •

Reformation Sunday is celebrated on the Sunday before All Saints' Day; it is most often the last Sunday in October. It celebrates the great reform movement in the church of the sixteenth century led by Martin Luther, Ulrich Zwingli, John Calvin, John Wycliff, and others. The Reformation was the beginning of the formation of many Protestant movements in the church, which dissented against some of the practices of the Roman Catholic Church. Justification by grace through faith was the central component of the Reformation movement. The importance of the Scriptures as the Word of God was also central, and it was from this concern that the Bible was first printed in the common language of the people rather than only in Latin.

Protestant denominations such as the United Church of Christ, Lutheran Church, Presbyterian Church, Moravian Church, and Baptist Church have their roots in the Reformation. Although each denomination is slightly different from the others in tradition and polity, they are all part of the reforming tradition of the church.

The lessons of the Reformation still hold importance for us today. The church of Jesus Christ is continually called to re-formation. In each new age, the church is called to examine itself in light of the world around it. The Spirit of God is constantly calling us to renewal.

The liturgical color for Reformation Sunday is red. Red signifies blood, to remind us of the martyrs of the faith who insisted that the church more clearly reflect what it means to be the Body of Christ.

Congregations celebrate Reformation Sunday by using the color red, singing songs, and reciting central teachings of the Reformation in their worship liturgies. An increasing number of churches celebrate the rite of confirmation on this day.

Many of us in this reform tradition do not know the history of the Reformation well. Reformation Sunday is an opportunity to find out more about this crucial time in church history and to reflect on its impact on the many Protestant traditions of the church. The stories of the leaders of the Reformation are part of our corporate church history. They can inform us about what it means to be a member of a reforming church today.

REFORMATION DAY PRAYER

(Light a red candle. If a red candle is not available, light a Christ candle.)
Transforming God, we remember and celebrate the great reformers of the Christian church in the Middle Ages. We remember Martin Luther, John Calvin, Ulrich Zwingli, John Wycliff, and many other women and men who were Reformation leaders. We give thanks for their courage and vision. We give thanks for all your prophets, visionaries, and martyrs, who down through the ages have constantly called the church to self-examination, change, and renewal.

We know that change is difficult. Your empowering Spirit continues to blow through our lives, our church, and our world. We are not always willing to confront the changes you call us to embrace. May we be attentive to your transforming power. May the church continue to strive to more fully reflect what it means to be the Body of Christ. We ask in the name of the One who came on your behalf and changed the world forever, our Savior, Jesus the Christ. Amen.

Sing: *(Sing one of the following hymns, or another that reflects the reforming nature of the church: "A Mighty Fortress," "We Would Be Building," "We Have This Ministry," etc. Such hymns can be found in most denominational hymnals.)*

• ALL SAINTS' DAY •

November 1 is the celebration of All Saints' Day. It is a day set aside to remember and celebrate people who have been examples of what it means to be followers of Jesus. It is no accident that this celebrating comes on the heels of Halloween. All Saints' Day was the church's response to the pagan rituals and beliefs surrounding All Hallows Eve.

All Saints' Day reminds us that we are part of the universal church of saints, the everlasting communion of believers, past, present, and future. The saints of God who have gone before us provide examples of what it means to witness on behalf of Christ. Throughout history there have been individuals and communities that exemplify being members of the body of Christ. All Saints' Day provides us with a time to remember these disciples and reflect about our own place in the universal church of Jesus Christ.

White is the liturgical color for All Saints' Day. Symbols include candles, crowns, and angels. Think about ways to use white and some of the symbols in your home celebration or dinner. Invite children to help you in making decorations or place settings. Consider some of these suggestions for making the day festive. Use white tablecloths, table runners, or place mats for a meal table. Light a Christ candle, baptismal candles, or another type of candle. Make table place cards in the shape of crowns for those gathered for a meal. Young children can make crowns for themselves to wear. These paper crowns can be decorated with pictures of how we can be followers of Jesus.

Parents of young children may want to take time, especially this day, to read Bible stories to their children. Story books about other people in history who exemplify Christian discipleship would also be appropriate. Discuss and share ideas about people who provide us with examples of Christian discipleship and servanthood.

I. LITURGY FOR ALL SAINTS' DAY
(Have a Christ candle, baptismal candles, or other candles available to light.)

Reader: Today is All Saints' Day. We remember the followers of Jesus in history who have shown us what it means to be a disciple. We light a candle to remember that by baptism we are all called to be saints of God.

(Light a Christ candle, baptismal candle, or other table candle.)

Reader: Hear these words from Scripture that help us to understand what being a follower of Jesus is like. (Read one of the following: Matthew 5:1–12; Ephesians 2:19–21; 5:8–10; 6:10–17; Colossians 3:12–17; 1 Peter 2:9–10.)

Reader: Let us name people in our past or present who are examples of saints of God.

(Name individuals in the Bible, history, your family, church, or community.)

Pray: **God of all generations, you are the God of Abraham and Sarah, Mary and Joseph, Paul and Lydia, and of so many others in history who have heard your call to discipleship. We give thanks for these ancestors of faith. May we seek to follow their example of obedience to your will. We give thanks for men and women in the present who witness to your way in this world. Bless us gathered today. Help us to remember that we are also called to reflect the light of Christ. By our baptisms you have chosen us to be your people—to be part of the household of the saints of God. May the continuing presence of your Spirit among us help us to live up to this calling. In the name of our Savior and Sovereign, Jesus the Christ. Amen.**

Sing: *(Sing an appropriate hymn for the day, such as "For All the Saints," "This Little Light of Mine," "I Sing a Song of the Saints of God," "When the Saints Go Marching In," etc.)*

II. Liturgy for All Saints' Day for Homes with Young Children

Reader: Today is a special day in the Christian church. Today is All Saints' Day. It is a day we remember and thank God for all the people who have shown us what it means to live the way God wants us to live. We remember people in the Bible. We remember people in history. We remember people in our family. We remember people in our church. We call these people saints of God.

Reader: We also remember Jesus. We remember what he taught us about living God's way. We light a special candle today to remember Jesus and to remember the people who follow the way of Jesus.

(Light a Christ candle.)

Reader: What names of people do we remember who have followed God's way?

(Name a few people.)

Reader: We also think about how we can be followers of Jesus today. How can we be followers of Jesus?

(Name a few ways to be followers of Jesus.)

Reader: Let us join hands and pray.
Gracious God, we thank you for all the people who have shown us what it means to live in your way. We especially thank you for Jesus. Help us to be good followers of Jesus too. Help us to become your saints. Amen.

III. A Prayer for All Saints' Day

God of power and grace, the world is filled this day with the light of your communion of saints. We thank you for all the saints, ancient and modern, who have gone before us and lit our journey of faith. May we learn by their example. Bless your servants gathered here. *(Name each individual who is present.)* **Grant us the courage to be your saints today. May we use the gifts you have given us to serve and witness to your Word in all we do. In this world of seeming gloominess, may we reflect the light of Christ in our lives. Bless our journeys of faith and grace us with your holy presence. In the name of Christ, the pioneer of our faith, our Savior, and your Word incarnate, we pray. Amen.**

IV. Celebration of Remembrance

Allow fifteen to thirty minutes for creativity and productivity. Set out pencils, crayons, markers, watercolors, paper, construction paper torn and cut into tiny mosaic tiles, and other items. String a clothesline across the dining area with clothespins to attach the "portraits" when completed.

Reader: Today we celebrate All Saints' Day, remembering people who have gone before us and those who are in our midst. These people have lived lives of faithfulness. Some are famous. Some are familiar. Let us remember.

(Have members of the family read sections of Hebrews 11. Choose one or two selections: verses 1–3, 4–7, 8–11, 17–22, 23–28, 29–31, 32–38, 39–40. Encourage children to read.)

Leader: Are there other people of faith whom we can remember today? Let us name some as we pray together.

Parent: O God, hear us as we pray for people of faith.

Youngest: We give thanks for teachers who help us learn to tie our shoes and tell time and learn times tables.

All: Thank you, God, for the patience of the saints.

Driver: We give thanks for the traffic cop who waves her hands and arms and makes sense out of tangled lanes of spaghetti traffic.

All: God, who led Miriam and Moses, who guided the footsteps of Ruth and Naomi, who nudged the reluctant disciples, we thank you for your guidance.

Parent: Thank you for the physician who listens, not only with a stethoscope, but also with a wise heart.

All: Healer, we give you thanks for all who heal.

Parent: Thank you for pastors and lay leaders who preach the Word and make stories of faith come alive.

All: God, who gave Jeremiah courage, who gave Priscilla confidence, who gave your Child as the living Word, thank you. Amen.

Now encourage each person to paint, draw, make a mosaic, or color a portrait of someone who lived by faith and made a lasting impression. When the portraits are completed, have each person tell the story of that saint. String the pictures across the room and keep the gallery of saints up for a few days. Remember them in your prayers each time you gather for a meal.

• HARVEST AND THANKSGIVING CELEBRATIONS •

There has always been a special time set aside during the faith calendar to give God thanks for all that God has done for us. This time of thanksgiving usually falls during the harvest season or toward the end of the Christian church year.

A meal is usually associated with this time of celebration. It can be a simple meal or formal meal. Involve a variety of people in preparing for your feast. Guests and family members can help prepare and bring food. Children can make place cards or settings as well as other decorations. Consider having music playing during your feast time to add to the festivities. Music that reflects the wonder of God's creation, the joy of living, and thanksgiving to God is most appropriate. Perhaps some people in your gathering can share their gifts of music. Singing a familiar hymn of thanksgiving can add to your celebration (for instance, "For the Beauty of the Earth," "Now Thank We All Our God," "Come, Ye Thankful People, Come," "We Gather Together").

If possible, use candles on your feast table to remind those gathered of the presence of Christ. Arrangements of flowers or other natural objects on the table can be reminders of the natural world and the bounty of creation.

Remember those in your church, workplace, or neighborhood who may not have a community of people to gather with for a thanksgiving feast. It is a long-standing tradition in the Bible to invite those in need of companionship to our meal tables.

I. A LITANY OF THANKSGIVING

(Use this litany before your meal. Have one or more people read the prayers of thanksgiving. If possible, include people of various ages as readers. Instruct all of those gathered to say the response, "Thank you, gracious God," after each petition.)

Reader: Most gracious God, from you comes every good and perfect gift. We gather here this day to remember your kindness and tender mercies that have filled the world since creation. We gather to give grateful thanksgiving with joy-filled hearts for all your bountiful gifts. From your womb comes forth the gift of life itself. For this we say,

Response:	Thank you, gracious God.
Reader:	The warmth of the sun and the gift of each new day. The quiet night and soft light of moon and stars that give us respite. The refreshing rain and the dancing of wind. For these we say,
Response:	Thank you, gracious God.
Reader:	The beauty and bounty of your creation. The gift of our senses to enjoy the wondrous and mysterious gift of life around us. The responsibility of stewardship of your garden earth. For these we say,
Response:	Thank you, gracious God.
Reader:	The work of our hands and hearts and minds. The gifts of the Spirit you bestow on each of us, known and as yet undiscovered. For these we say,
Response:	Thank you, gracious God.
Reader:	The gift of family relationships. The love of husband and wife. The joy and insights of children. The wisdom and truth of our elders. The companionship of coworkers, friends, and neighbors. The discipline, joy, and struggle of living in covenant with one another. For these we say,
Response:	Thank you, gracious God.
Reader:	The One who has shown us the way of your truth and righteousness in this world. The Savior who has conquered death. The gift of Emmanuel—God with us—Jesus the Christ. For this we say,
Response:	Thank you, gracious God.
Reader:	Accept the grateful thanksgiving of our humble hearts. For all that we have named, and for so much more that we have left unnamed, we give you thanks. Come, gracious Creator, Savior, and Sustainer. Be with us in our feasting and celebration this day. Amen.

II. A TABLE LITURGY OF THANKSGIVING

(Instruct those gathered for the meal to sit or stand around the table. Have one or two candles on the table. If possible, invite several people to be readers for the liturgy.)

Reader: We gather at this feast to take time from our busy lives to give thanks to our God. We greet this feast with humble, joy-filled hearts. May the light of these candles remind us of the gift of the light of Christ in our lives. May we always reflect that light.

(Light the candles on the table.)

Reader: We remember that our biblical ancestors set aside time each year to give thanks to God for God's graciousness and stead-fast love. Jesus sat at the table with friends and strangers and blessed the goodness of God's bounty. Our Native American brothers and sisters gave generously of food and knowledge to our Pilgrim mothers and fathers that they might survive in a new land. Today we recall all that God has done for us.

Reader: *(Read one of the following: Psalm 8, 111, 145, 146, 148.)*

Reader: Let us take time to reflect silently or to offer in words the gifts that God has given us.

(Allow those gathered to offer verbally their thanksgiving, or allow time for silent reflection.)

Reader: Let us remember those who cannot be with us at this table.

(Allow a few moments for silent reflection or spoken remembrances of persons who are not present.)

Reader: Let us remember those in need of God's care. Those who are hungry, poor, homeless, struggling with life, sick and alone.

(Allow a moment of silence.)

Reader: Gracious Provider, it is from you that all good gifts come. Hear our grateful praise to you this day. Send your Spirit to join us in our feasting and celebration. And when this day is done, remind us to be a daily reflection of your gracious compassion and steadfast love. By our words and deeds we witness to your way and truly give you our thanks. In the name of Jesus Christ we pray. Amen.

III. A THANKSGIVING BLESSING
(Use several readers for this blessing.)

Pray: Holy Provider, we gather to celebrate the gifts of life that you have graciously bestowed upon us. Be with us this day and bless those who have gathered at this feast.

Reader: Bless the hands that have prepared and worked to provide this table that nourishes not only our bodies, but also our spirits. Bless those gathered here today, those who have journeyed far and those who live nearby.

Reader: Bless our children. May they continue to grow in the warmth of your light and know of your steadfast love for them.

Reader: Bless our teenagers. May they know that true wisdom and identity of soul come from knowing you.

Reader: Bless those here journeying in adult life. May their work and play always reflect the gifts of your Spirit deep within them.

Reader: Bless our elders. May their experience and wisdom offer to us all hope for the journey of life and faith.

Reader: Bless friends, family, and loved ones who cannot join us in our feast. May they know of our love and of your presence.

Reader: Bless this celebration of thanksgiving. In the midst of our preparations and expectations, our loud voices and quiet pain, our conflict and camaraderie, and our joy and weariness at the end of this day, bless our lives in all our wonder and frailty. Know that deep within us we are grateful for your steadfast love and enduring grace in our lives. Amen.

• REIGN OF CHRIST SUNDAY •

Reign of Christ Sunday is the last Sunday in the Christian year. It is a day set aside to celebrate that Christ is the one who rules over all time—past, present, and future. This church year may be coming to a close, but God's history continues to unfold from age to age, spiraling into the future. For family worship, meditation on the reign of Christ presents exciting challenges, opportunities for discussion and service.

CELEBRATION OF CHRIST'S REIGN

Read together the scene of the Great Judgment from Matthew 25:31–46. Encourage people to make notes as the passage is read aloud. Ask the young children to draw pictures instead of writing. What are the signs of faithfulness that are named in this passage (feeding the hungry, clothing the naked, welcoming the stranger, caring for the sick, visiting those in prison)? Take some time to remember when, over the course of the past year, you engaged in these holy tasks. Help one another as you recall together visiting a nursing home, stocking the food pantry, calling on a new neighbor, or contributing to a mission at church.

When the lists are finished, have each person read the list aloud, and at the conclusion of each reading, all say, "We were serving Christ when we did those things!"

Then make a list of the new ways you plan to be in ministry in the coming year. Be bold in your predictions, and ask family members to bolster your courage and hold you accountable.

Again, read the lists, concluding each time with the short prayer, "May we serve Christ when we do these things!"

Finally, reflect on the ways you have fallen short of the expectation to live life in service to the least of these. After a period of silent reflection, light the Christ candle, and offer this prayer or one like it:

Christ, in your mercy, forgive us for the ways we have failed as disciples.

God, in your tenderness, reach out to all who suffer or are lonely or hungry.

Spirit, in your wisdom, make us strong for the tasks of ministry ahead. Amen.

PRAYER FOR REIGN OF CHRIST SUNDAY

Timekeeper of eternity, we come to the close of another church year. It has been a year filled with joy and sadness, with possibilities and dashed hopes, with hope and despair. As we have journeyed through this year, you have been our constant mark, our compass leading us home. Guide us again in the time before us. Help us to keep the rhythm of the faith, day in and day out. May we mark the seasons not by minutes, hours, days, or weeks, but by words said and deeds done on behalf of Christ, our Sovereign and Savior. Amen.

SEASONAL CELEBRATIONS

We live not only according to the church year, but also according to a cultural and seasonal calendar. Special days throughout the yearly calendar permit us to recognize the heritage of our country, cultural and ancient heroes, the importance of play and feasting, the significance of special people in our lives, and the natural rhythms of nature. Some of these holidays do not seem to be intimately connected with the life of faith. Yet everything in our lives is infused with the sacred nature of life and the Divine Creator. We may at times feel that we live in two worlds. These prayers and liturgies help us to remember that even in secular and cultural celebrations the presence of God is near.

New Year's Eve and New Year's Day

I. NEW YEAR'S EVE CELEBRATION

You will need the following items: ten candles of any variety, matches, and music ("Auld Lang Syne" or "Morning Has Broken" or "I Was There to Hear Your Borning Cry"). If you have young children, you may want to plan this event for 7:00 P.M. and then put the kids to bed. If you are doing this with young children, you may prepare some note cards with scripture texts or pictures on them for each child to choose one.

During the evening of New Year's Eve, instruct each member of the family to write down ten things from the past year for which he or she is thankful. As the hour of midnight approaches, invite each person to find a Bible passage to launch the New Year. Read one of the following scriptures or another appropriate one: Ecclesiastes 3; Psalm 1; Isaiah 43; Romans 8; 1 Thessalonians.

At ten minutes to midnight, gather the family around the ten candles. As each minute ticks down, light one candle and have each person read the ten items on the list created earlier.

When midnight tolls, have each person read the Bible verse that he or she has chosen for the new year.

Pray: O Ancient One, gather up our thanks for times gone by.
             O God of newness, receive our praise for the dawn of
             another year.
             Holy One, bless us as we move into the new year.
             We pray in the name of Christ, who makes all things new.
             Amen.

Sing a song: *(Choose one listed above or another that is appropriate for the
             celebration.)*

Eat: Share a midnight breakfast.

II. New Year's Eve Liturgy

Read: *(Read Ecclesiastes 3:1–8.)*

Pray: Keeper of all times and seasons, we greet this new year
             with anticipation as well as apprehension. We do not
             know what this journey of days, weeks, months, and sea-
             sons holds for us. Go before us and guide our way. Open
             us to the excitement and possibility of each morning. Give
             us rest and reassurance in the gentle veil of each night.
             Help us to use the time you have given us in ways that
             truly reflect your intentions for our lives. We ask in the
             name of the one who is the ruler of all eternity, Christ our
             Savior. Amen.

III. New Year's Eve Liturgy

Setting: The basement, garage, or spare room.

Materials: Candles, a Christ candle, empty boxes, recycling bins,
             cleaning supplies.

Liturgy and Celebration

Family members gather at an agreed upon time in the designated "clean-
out" spot.

The liturgy (which literally means "work of the people") works back-
ward from midnight (or the appropriate hour if celebrating with young-
sters or elderly family members). Saving fifteen minutes for the end,
calculate how much can be accomplished. Then let the cleaning begin!

Develop a system for tossing, keeping, and giving away, perhaps with
different boxes and accompanying sound effects to go with each decision.
Try this:

"Crash, bang, bong, the old is gone!" is the cheer for tossing things into the throwaway box.

"Treasures for the keeping, memories in the making!" is the cry for saving articles with the intention of using, rearranging, or putting them in a scrapbook.

"Love grows as these things go!" is the rallying cry for items to be donated to charity—a shelter, halfway house, church rummage sale, or Goodwill.

Include all ages so that little ones might carry things to the designated boxes or frail elderly members could provide the music or refresh glasses or snacks.

Make a ceremony out of cleaning—dance with the mops, Fred Astaire–style, exaggerate scrubbing, turn up the joyful music, and get the blood flowing as you exorcise the "demons of dirt" and prepare for the new year.

LITANY OF REMEMBERING AND NEW BEGINNINGS

(Set up candles on a newly cleaned surface, making sure that all debris is out of the way. Place the Christ candle in the center. Light all the candles but the Christ candle.)

One Voice:	Let this be a holy place, O God. May the basement *(or appropriate room)* of our house be uncluttered, and the foundation of our faith be resting in you.
All:	Bless this space.
One Voice:	Help us to enter the new year with uncluttered hearts. Clear away the cobwebs of doubt or despair, wash away the mistakes of the past, and open us to the possibilities you have in store for us.
All:	Bless us in the new year.

(Light the Christ candle.)

One Voice:	We light the Christ candle to remind us of our center point, the center of our household.
All:	Make us mindful of Christ's presence. Help us to keep our house open to his message of reconciliation and love. And let the new year begin with Christ as our light. Amen!

NEW YEAR'S DAY LITURGY

(Ahead of time provide glasses for all gathered to share in a toast. Make sure there are appropriate beverages for all to drink. Light a Christ candle or another candle to signify the presence of Christ.)

Reader: We gather to thank God for the past year. We put it aside with all of its blessings and struggles. We gather to greet and anticipate the new year. We may be filled with hopes and dreams as well as fears and hesitations. Whatever our hopes and fears are for the next twelve months, we are assured that God will take care of us.

Reader: *(Read Psalm 121.)*

Reader: If you are willing, share with us what you hope for this coming year.

(Give those gathered an opportunity to share.)

Pray: **God, our strength and stronghold, you have seen fit to bring us through this past year with all its joys and sorrows. We give you thanks. Be with us as we enter this new year. Receive our hopes and wipe away our fears. May we begin this new year with joy and anticipation. Be with us in this celebration and bless us in the days ahead. Amen.**

(Invite those assembled to raise a glass honoring the new year.)

A HOUSE BLESSING FOR THE NEW YEAR

O Holy God, bless this house and all who live within its walls. Bless our coming in and going out from this dwelling. As we journey in the year ahead, may we be sent forth from this place as beacons of your light and hope. When we return, may we find sanctuary and safety. May this house always be filled with love and grace, compassion and forgiveness, joy and laughter. May our sorrows diminish in the shelter of each other's presence. May we learn the value of work and play. May those who enter as guests find warmth and gracious hospitality. Protect and guide, O God, all those who find a home in this place. Keep us in your tender care in the days to come. Amen.

Martin Luther King Jr. Day

January 15 is the birthday of Dr. Martin Luther King Jr. Dr. King and his leadership in the civil rights movement of the 1960s show us a clear example of Christian discipleship in the modern world. Dr. King's life and work were shaped by his strong roots in the biblical tradition that testified to the liberating power of God in Christ.

Dr. King's birthday provides us with an opportunity to tell the story of his life and ministry. This might be done during a family meal. Consider reading aloud parts of his powerful speeches. Discuss how family members are living out their call to Christian discipleship in light of Dr. King's example.

PRAYER FOR JUSTICE

Liberating and saving God, today we remember and give thanks for the life of Dr. Martin Luther King Jr. By prophetic words and actions, he witnessed to your vision of a just and righteous world. In his insistence on nonviolence, he exemplified the power of love to change the world. His life reminds us that one person can indeed make a difference. Help us to learn from Dr. King's example. Give us the imagination to dream dreams of a better world. Grant us the courage to be able to speak out for justice and equality. Make our hearts beat with compassion for all humanity. In the name of the one who calls us to sacrificial servanthood on behalf of others, Jesus Christ. Amen.

Valentine's Day

Valentine's Day falls on the feast day of two third-century Christian martyrs, each named Valentine. The holiday also incorporates ancient Roman customs associated with romance. Tradition says that one of the Valentines sent a note to the jailer's daughter the night before his death and signed it "from your Valentine." Other stories mention the love between Valentine and this young woman. Still others say that the imprisoned Valentine received notes from those who supported and cared for him. Valentine's Day can be a delightful reminder of how we care for those close to us. It can also remind us of our call to love others on behalf of Christ. Despite the modern commercialism of this holiday, we can find simple ways of sharing our love and care for family, friends, and strangers.

Before Valentine's Day, cut out red construction paper hearts for each member of your family. Write a brief note on each one, and leave the heart where each member will find it sometime during the day (lunch boxes, coat pockets, dresser, etc.). Each individual can do this for the other family members.

Plan a special meal. Decorate the table with a red tablecloth, use red place mats or a red table runner, or arrange a few red flowers. Light a candle to remind you of Christ's presence. Put a construction paper heart at each person's place. On the heart write a verse from the Bible about love (e.g., Deut. 6:5; Mark 12:31a; John 3:16; 1 Cor. 13:4, 5, 7). During your meal, discuss what these verses mean for you as Christians. Invite friends and extended family to share your meal. Ask everyone to bring a part of the meal to share. Consider inviting people who may be alone.

Make or buy heart-shaped cookies. As a family, deliver them to neighbors and individuals who are unable to leave their homes. Write letters (or draw pictures) to those who might be in need of your concern. In the Valentine tradition, send mail to people such as church missionaries, pen pals, hospital patients, nursing home residents, and college students.

PRAYER FOR THE GIFTS OF LOVE

God of infinite and steadfast love, today we are reminded of the gifts of love. Love that comes from you. Love that is felt between those gathered. Love that is shared with others. Love that is given to those we do not know but who are in need of our compassion. Love that is showered upon us in numerous ways. We thank you for your steadfast love, even though we do not always return it. Remind us that it is in loving others that we truly show our love for you. In the name of Jesus Christ, the clearest example of your holy love, we pray. Amen.

NAMING PRAYER

In this prayer individuals will have an opportunity to give thanks for those who have shown them love. Individuals can take turns by saying, "I give thanks for _____." Or a leader can say, "We give thanks for _____," and each person can name individuals.

God of all love, we give you thanks this day for those who surround us with examples of your love and compassion. *(We give you thanks for/I give you thanks for) (allow those gathered to express their thanks for those who love them).* For all these people who grace us with their love, we give you thanks. As we have been blessed by their love, may we bless others with our love. In the name of love made flesh, Jesus Christ. Amen.

Saint Patrick's Day

Saint Patrick's Day falls on March 17. Many stories surround this man who is said to have brought Christianity to Ireland about the fifth century. Celebrating Saint Patrick's Day is not reserved just for the Irish or descendants of Irish people. It is a fun holiday enjoyed by many people.

Wearing green clothing, eating Irish foods, and sharing stories of mischievous leprechauns are some of the delightful traditions that surround this day. Serving Irish soda bread, corned beef and cabbage, or Irish stew is a fun way to join in the festivities.

The many stories of leprechauns are amusing to share with children. When our children were young, they would awaken to find that leprechauns had been in the house during the night. Furniture was misplaced, and other things were out of order. The "little people" also left gold in the form of gold paper–wrapped candy throughout the house.

The story of Patrick is not clear, as is true with the stories of many of our ancient ancestors. We do know that he composed lovely blessings and prayers. The prayer below is believed to have been written on Patrick's breastplate. Amid your Saint Patrick's Day merriment, use this prayer to begin and end the day, or at mealtime. It is a reminder that Christ is ever present in our lives.

A PRAYER OF SAINT PATRICK

Christ be with me. Christ within me, Christ behind me, Christ before me, Christ beside me, Christ to win me, Christ to comfort and restore me, Christ above me, Christ beneath me, Christ in quiet, Christ in danger, Christ in hearts of all that love me, Christ in mouth of friend and stranger. Amen.

Mother's Day

LITANY FOR MOTHERS

(After each petition, have those gathered respond with, "We thank you, mothering God." If possible, use several people to read the petitions.)

Reader: Mothering God, we give thanks this day for all the mothers we have known in our lives. For *(names of mothers)* who nourished us in the womb and gave us birth,

Response: We thank you, mothering God.

Reader: For our mothers who loved us, nurtured us, and guided our steps through childhood into the adult world, for *(names of mothers)*.

Response: We thank you, mothering God.

Reader: For all those women in our lives who have been like a mother, for grandmothers, aunts, cousins, friends, and neighbors,

Response: We thank you, mothering God.

Reader: For all the women in our history and in our current lives who have served as role models and mentors and thus have mothered us,

Response: We thank you, mothering God.

Reader: Nurturing and loving God, we give thanks for the mothers in our lives whom you have given us. Bless them and keep them in your care. Make us worthy of their investment in our lives. Help us to honor them and you by leading lives centered in compassionate discipleship. Amen.

MOTHER'S DAY PRAYER

Mothering God, we give you thanks for the gift of (name of mother) in our lives. In her compassionate care for us, she has shown us what it means to give of oneself in love. For the countless known and unknown tasks she has done for us, for the countless ways she has mothered and mentored us, for her strength and courage, for the laughter and tears spent on our behalf, for all the ways in which she has given us life, we give thanks.

Grant her your continued blessing and presence. Make us mindful of all she has done and continues to do for us. In the name of your love made flesh, Jesus Christ, we pray. Amen.

Festival of the Christian Home

In some churches, the traditional Mother's Day has become the Festival of the Christian Home. Here is a prayer that celebrates the home and the vocation of homemaking. It may also be used on Father's Day.

PRAYER

Holy God, dwelling place of all generations, today we celebrate the gift of home. We give thanks for those people and places in our lives that have provided us with a sheltering and nurturing presence. We celebrate and give thanks for mothers and fathers, family and friends, who provide homes that are centered in your steadfast love. Thank you for their diligence in homemaking. For safe places to grow, to learn, to cry, to laugh, to work, and to play, we give thanks. For nourishment of body and soul, for rest from the weariness of the world, we give thanks.

We remember those as well who do not have healthy homes in which to live. Be with them and let your gracious presence be known in the midst of turmoil. Like an eagle, protect us and all of your children under your warm and sheltering wings. Bless our home. Bless all those who enter and depart from its protective sheltering. May they find compassionate hearts and hospitable hands patterned after your divine image. Amen.

Memorial Day

Memorial Day is a poignant call to remember persons who lost their lives in pursuit of peace. Regardless of political persuasion or patriotic inclinations, we are called to attention on this day. Civil ceremonies abound, from wreath planting to gun salutes. How does a family celebrate this bittersweet day of mixed metaphors?

It is an ideal day to address ambiguities, to name differences and diversity within a family, to honor those who have died, and to remember the One who makes us whole. Before a picnic or prior to liftoff on a trip, in the quiet of the morning or the cool of the evening, take time for a liturgy at home.

Place in the middle of the table the Christ candle, stars cut out in silver or gold, pictures of family members who have died in the wars, gardening tools (to represent the transformation of weapons into plowshares and pruning hooks), and small plants, seedlings, or shrubs to be planted.

MEMORIAL DAY LITURGY
(Light the candle and enter into this liturgy.)

One Voice: On this day, O God of peace, we confess that we often fall short of your vision for us. We raise weapons to resolve conflicts; we rear our children to fight their way out of problems.

All: Help us to be peacemakers.

One Voice: On this day, O Healer, we remember all who have fallen in battle, all who sacrificed their lives for the causes they held dear.

All: Heal our memories and comfort us.

One Voice: On this day, O God of promise, we commit ourselves to lives of peace.

All: We pledge allegiance to the Bringer of Peace, Jesus Christ. Amen.

After the prayer, extinguish the candle and go outside to plant a peace garden. You may wish to dedicate your plantings to someone's memory. You may want to take the plantings to an inner-city park, a nursing home, your church, or a playground to brighten another corner of your world. As you work together you may want to talk about peaceful problem solving, alternative methods for conflict resolution, and creative ways to deal with the increase of violence around us. Listen for ideas from the children and honor their opinions and experiences.

PRAYER FOR THOSE WHO DIED IN A WAR
(Use this prayer if the family visits a graveyard to decorate the grave of a loved one.)

O God of life, you are older than time. You have seen generations snuffed out by sacrifice, by war, by courage, and by folly. You have comforted generations who mourned and grieved and sang solemn songs

and laid flowers on graves. Gather us, too, in your embrace and cradle us with your compassion. As we remember *(name),* help us to remember that you were there when the mountains were formed, you were there to soothe the grief and breathe hope into the hopeless, and you are with us still, in the stillness of this moment. We give you thanks for life in Jesus Christ and pray that our lives may be reflections of his love. Amen.

TABLE PRAYER FOR MEMORIAL DAY

(Place the Christ candle in the middle of the table, and place red, white, and blue ribbons on the table.)

Youngest:	O God, today we remember people who have died fighting for a cause in which they believed.
Oldest:	*(Lights the Christ candle.)* O God, we remember the call to peace that comes from the Bringer of Peace.
All:	Help us to stand up for what we believe. Help us to stand up for peace. And help the world to find ways to live without wars. Amen.
Youngest:	O God, we pray for all who have been victims of wars they did not start or did not want.
Oldest:	For lost land, ruined villages, shattered dreams, and divided families, we grieve the waste and the scars.
All:	Lover of Peace, heal our broken world and mend our hearts. Amen.

(People may add prayers for loved ones who have died or who are grieving the loss of another.)

Read:	*(Read Psalm 90:1–2.)*

(Sit in silence for a minute.)

Oldest:	Amen! God is with us.

NIGHTTIME PRAYER FOR MEMORIAL DAY

We close our day hearing the echo of the haunting refrain of music in graveyards, feeling the weight of mantelpieces heavy with old photographs, reeling with stories of sacrifice—unwitting, unwilling, unwavering. We remember strategists, soldiers, planners, and pilots. We are weary of war and the toll it takes on your people, O God. We pray for the day when the swords are turned into plowshares and the spears into pruning hooks. We long for the day when we will harvest in the garden of peace. Now send us into our rest with dreams of peace and tunes of harmony as our lullabies. Amen.

Father's Day

LITANY FOR FATHER'S DAY

(Have those gathered respond after each prayer petition with, "We thank you, fathering God." Invite several people to be readers.)

Reader: Fathering God, we take time today to celebrate and give thanks for all those who have fathered us. For our own fathers (names of fathers), who have given us life and rejoice at our birth,

Response: We thank you, fathering God.

Reader: For those men in our lives who have nurtured us and mentored us, who have played and worked with us, who have provided warmth and safety for us,

Response: We thank you, fathering God.

Reader: For those men who are like a father to us, for grandfathers, uncles, cousins, friends, and neighbors,

Response: We thank you, fathering God.

Reader: For men who were our forefathers and for current fathers who provide role models of what it means to father in compassionate, caring, and loving ways,

Response: We thank you, fathering God.

Reader: Bless these fathers in our lives. Grant them your continued presence and guidance. May we honor them with our lips, but even more so in living lives centered in your loving way. In the name of Christ, who called you Abba. Amen.

A FATHER'S DAY PRAYER

Fathering God, who gives us gracious, compassionate love, we thank you for the gift of *(name of father)*. For his compassion and caring, for his wisdom and humility, for his strength and courage, for his mentoring and role modeling, for the laughter and tears spent on our behalf, we give thanks. May we honor his presence in our lives, and all he has done for us, by living a life worthy of his call to fatherhood. May we follow your way of steadfast loving as *(name of father)* has done. Bless *(name of father)* and continue to be present in his life, in times of joy and times of trial. We ask in the name of Jesus Christ, our brother and Savior. Amen.

Fourth of July

The Fourth of July is often filled with picnics and parades. Maybe prayer has not been a part of the celebration for your family. Perhaps a touch of prayerful picnicking or joyful parading would be in order! Use the picnic motif to reinforce the theme of feasting and hospitality that is so prevalent in the Hebrew Scriptures and the Gospel stories. As you pack the picnic basket, drop in some prayers of thanksgiving to be read at the table.

Many of the men and women who founded this country did so out of a deep faith perspective. We often forget this in our festivities. During your celebration, consider having the Declaration of Independence read aloud for all to hear. Or read other documents from the early history of the United States that speak to this holiday. For instance, read Emma Lazarus's poem "The New Colossus," which appears on the Statue of Liberty, or excerpts from speeches by Martin Luther King Jr. or other freedom fighters.

As evening comes and sparklers are lit, you may wish to use that ceremony as one to remember the many freedoms we celebrate. Consider the many cultures and ethnic groups making up the United States. You may also use the sparklers to remember martyrs for freedom such as Martin Luther King Jr., Cesar Chavez, Harriet Tubman, Sojourner Truth, or persons in your community who may be working to ensure freedoms and civil rights for all. Dance with the sparklers as you remember their names and stories. Sing "America the Beautiful." End your day with a prayer.

PRAYERS

Thank you, God, for freedom and fireworks. Thank you for ice cream and watermelon. Make us mindful of those who struggle to be free. Make us aware of ways that our lives and decisions limit the freedom of others. As the night sky is illuminated by fireworks, may we remember the ways that you light the way for us, that you delight us with the splendor of the night skies, and that you surprise us with awesome displays of your presence. As the stories of freedom and courage are told today, make us bold enough to be revolutionary in our faith. Help us to pursue liberty and justice, not just for ourselves, but for all. We pray in the name of the One who gives us courage, who claims us, feeds us, and frees us, Jesus Christ. Amen.

— or —

Liberating God, we give you thanks for this wondrous country in which we live. We give you thanks that you have guided us to this point in our history. Remind us of our heritage—a heritage that invites and includes all people into this country. In our hearts we hold the stories of those who have struggled to help this country live up to its ideals. Do not let us forget this heritage. Deliver us from arrogance. Help us remember that you are the God of all nations. We are called to not be so proud as to forget that we are one nation among many nations in your care. Thank you for the excitement and fun of this day. Bless us on our continued journey as your people, a people gifted with the splendors of this country. Amen.

Labor Day

Labor Day has been transformed from a holiday honoring work and workers into an end-of-summer ritual. It is a kind of New Year's Day, finding us with one foot in the more carefree days of summer and one foot in the schedule and structure of September. The rhythm of work and leisure may vary as your life situation changes. Maybe you are getting ready for school, taking one last camping trip, or cleaning out the closets. Wherever you may find yourselves, take time for a liturgy about labor. Rest and consider the role of work in your lives. It might be an opportunity to ask parents and grandparents about the jobs and vocations they have had in their lives. Did they have a paper route in their youth? Was Grandpa ever a soda jerk? And what is that anyway?

Talk with adolescents about the values you take to the workplace. Role-play some workday situations with them, and help them to see the ways that your faith goes with you, no matter what work you do. Dream about work yet to be accomplished. You could make a commitment to reassess your roles with a spouse. Who gets the next vocational move? Are the double shifts taking their toll on your relationship? How are layoffs affecting your family? Dream big, listen with compassion, and find some way to honor work in your day.

MORNING PRAYER

Creator God, thank you for doing your job this morning. For lifting the veil of night and painting the sky with daytime hues. Help us to do our jobs this morning. The job of living peaceably in the family, the jobs around the house or yard that may seem like drudgery but have moments of grace, the job of celebrating your presence in small things. Make us mindful of all sorts and conditions of folks who work or wish they did.

(Then pray one of these endings to prayer:)

Comforter God, be with the police officers, the nurses, the service personnel, the doctors, the resort owners, the burger flippers, the housekeepers, and other persons who labor today while others play. Amen.

– or –

Home of the sparrow, be with those who are homeless, with those who have no jobs to complain about or no work that brings meaning and challenge. Amen.

– or –

Source of meaning, help us to find our meaning in you, that drawing from your well, we might be ready for the tasks that face us. Guide us and guard us this day. We pray in Christ's name. Amen.

EVENING PRAYER

Great God, we thank you for this day. As the colors fade from the sky and the comforter of the evening is resting on us, we appreciate this labor of your love. We thank you for the subtleties of your work: the unique characteristics of the people around us, the multicolored, richly diverse faces of people around us, the wild array of flowers and trees and animals, the singular sounds of summer sidewalks—hopscotch, boom boxes, spurting flumes from water hydrants, footsteps. We pray for safety and rest and shelter for all who are in your care. Comfort those who suffer tonight. Help us to work to bring about a just society to match the splendors of your creation. Then we will rest our weary heads and hear your benediction, "Well done, good and faithful servants." Amen.

Beginning of the School Year

The beginning of a new school year is a big transition in families with children who go to school. The mixture of events that this time of year brings—facing the end of summer and returning to a regular routine, meeting new teachers and going to new classes, seeing old friends and making new ones—provides a mixture of emotions.

NEW SCHOOL YEAR LITURGY

Read: This candle reminds us of the presence of Christ. It also reminds us that the wisdom and knowledge of God are like a light in our lives.

(Light a candle.)

Read: *(One person or several people can read Psalm 119:33–48.)*

Pray: **God of all true wisdom and knowledge, we are at the beginning of another school year. Be with us in the hours, days, weeks, and months ahead. Open our hearts and minds, our eyes and ears, to the miracle of everything in your creation. Engage our imaginations and souls so that we might see beyond the written facts and figures. Do not let us be satisfied with what we already know. Help us to struggle with new knowledge, and give us patience when we cannot understand. Be with the teachers and administrators in our schools. Guide them in their work. Be with us in the activities surrounding school. In working or playing with our friends, give us a cooperative and compassionate spirit. Amid all of the knowledge we shall gain this year, remind us that the teachings of Jesus are central to who we are as your people. Let the presence of your awakening Spirit guide us in the year ahead. In the name of our teacher, friend, and Savior, Jesus Christ. Amen.**

PRAYER FOR A NEW SCHOOL YEAR

(Before reading this prayer, gather together the night before school begins. Encourage family members to share what they are excited, sad, and concerned about for the days ahead.)

God of all times and seasons, we give you thanks for the season of summer. It is over too soon. We are not sure we are ready to begin this school year. Help us to look forward to this year of study and growth in knowledge. Give us open minds and hearts to what lies ahead. Remind us that you are the God of the past, present, and future. Assure us that as you were with us in the past year, you will be with us in the school year ahead. Let us be ever mindful that in whatever joys and struggles we have this year, you are with us. Bless us in the journey ahead. Amen.

THE FIRST DAY OF SCHOOL

(Use this prayer for a young child at the beginning of preschool or kindergarten.)
Dear God, be with me today as I go to school. Help me to learn new things. Help my ears to listen, my eyes to see, and my hands to work. Teach me to share and care for other people. Bless my teacher and all the children in my class. Amen.

(Read this prayer the morning before everyone leaves for school.)
O God, as we begin this first day of school, we ask that you be with us. We are excited to see old friends. We are curious about new students and teachers. We are scared by the unknown day that lies ahead. Help us to be brave and face this new day. Help us to remember that we are not alone. You are always with us even if we do not feel your presence. Bless us and all those in school this day. In the name of our friend and Savior, Jesus the Christ. Amen.

A PRAYER FOR TEEN STUDENTS

Mysterious God, Creator of the universe, remind us that we are made in your image, that you have given us inquisitive minds, a creative imagination to be used in seeking knowledge. Prod us to question and doubt. Help us to see that beyond textbooks and chalkboards, there is a deeper truth to life's meaning. No matter how confused and challenged we are with growing and learning, grant us the reassurance that you are present in our searchings. May we have gifted and caring teachers and mentors from the past and present to guide us. Bless us as we continue to become the persons you intend for us to be. In the name of Jesus, your wisdom made flesh, we pray. Amen.

A PRAYER BEFORE LEAVING HOME FOR STUDY

(This may be said at a special family meal given before the student leaves.)
God of new journeys, we remember that throughout history your people have journeyed to unknown places and toward unknown events. We remember that in all of their adventures, you were present. You guided, protected, prodded, and cared for your people. Be with *(name)* as *(he/she)* begins a school year away from this home. Grant safe passage to *(her/his)* new dwelling place.

Send *(her/him)* out into this new beginning with courage and hopefulness. Help *(her/him)* with the new experiences *(he/she)* will encounter. Remind *(her/him)* that there are others around to help when needed. Give *(her/him)* wise and caring teachers, compassionate and trusted companions. In all *(name)* will encounter, remind *(her/him)* of who *(he/she)* is—one of your chosen people, marked by baptism. Let *(her/him)* know of your constant and steadfast love, and of the love of *(her/his)* family. Bless the journey ahead, and bring *(name)* safely back to us in good time filled with new knowledge and understanding of life. In the name of Jesus the Christ we pray. Amen.

Travel and Vacations

We are a people on the move. Our world gets smaller and travel gets easier. Business and vacations may take us on the road, in the air, or through the water. We anticipate these times with joy and apprehension. God's people have always been on the go. Where we go—God goes too!

A PRAYER BEFORE BEGINNING A TRIP

God of the traveler, we ask that your presence be with us on our journey. Go before us and lead our way. May our minds be open to the wonders along our route. In whatever we encounter may we know of your presence. May the strangers we meet be gracious and hospitable. May we in turn be gracious to all we meet. Grant us a safe journey to our destination. Keep us from harm's way. At the end of our journey, may we give you thanks for guiding our path. As you have been with all your people in their journeys, be with us at the beginning, middle, and end of our trip. Amen.

A PRAYER FOR A TIME OF RECREATION

God of Sabbath, you rested from your work of creation. You delight in our times of play and recreation. Be present with us in this time of rest and relaxation. Help us to realize the joy of being part of your creation.

Teach us to slow down and enjoy each day of this time away. May this be a time of respite from work and responsibilities. May this be a time of renewal for our bodies and spirits. Grant us a safe journey to our destination. Help us to truly make this time a time of Sabbath. Amen.

A PRAYER BEFORE BEGINNING A FAMILY VACATION

As we begin this holiday time together, O God, we ask for your presence, guidance, and blessing. We live scattered lives throughout the year. May this time together bring us closer as a family. We often take one another for granted. May we find renewed joy in one another's presence.

We do not take time in our busy lives to see the beauty around us. May we experience together the wonder of your creation. We often forget the strength we have as a family. May we realize in being together on this adventure the strong bonds of our companionship. In the name of our brother and Savior, Jesus Christ. Amen.

TRAVELING LITURGY

Sometimes on vacations or trips the days blend into one another, and the memories seem like blurred scenery out the window of a moving car or train. Mindfulness on the journey is a great metaphor for life and easy to learn while traveling.

Assign a different person the role of recorder for each day of a trip. The recorder writes down a journal entry or draws a picture of significant events, observations, and/or sights on the day's travel. At the close of the day, invite that person to compose a prayer about those things.

For example, the child writes down notes about seeing a homeless person on the street, taking a ride at an amusement park, seeing a beautiful sunset, and being scared about losing the car keys. As the child recounts each thing, the family responds: "God was with us," or "Make us mindful." Here is an example.

One:	For the guy I saw on the street today with all his things wrapped up in blankets,
All:	Make us mindful, O God.
One:	When we were falling out of the sky on the roller coaster,
All:	God was with us.
One:	When we were afraid that we had lost the car keys,

All:	God was with us.
One:	For the beautiful sunset,
All:	Make us mindful, O God.

These notes, pictures, and prayers could be part of the memorabilia in the scrapbook about the trip. Or the family could keep a travel journal and add to it on successive trips. To keep track of it, store it in a suitcase that always goes along on trips.

LITURGY FOR THE SOLO TRAVELER

Solo travel can be disorienting. Being on the road pulls you off center. It is difficult to feel at home in hotel room after motel room. Ancient people often had more portable rituals, complete with symbols or icons that created a worship space. We may consider this to be archaic and impractical. You could not fit the ark of the covenant "in the space under the seat in front of you or in the overhead bins"!

Travel liturgy may seem a private piety that misses the point of the communal nature of prayer and worship. And yet it may be a way of getting centered again after a day of airports or conferences or conventions or car travel. Keep these items packed in your suitcase or overnight kit:

··· A couple of votive candles and holders (a variety of inexpensive holders are available, many of which cast interesting shadows on the sterile walls of a nondescript hotel room)
··· Cloth (a fabric remnant, scarf, woven place mat, particularly in the liturgical season's color)
··· A favorite devotional book of daily readings or a prayer book, a blank prayer journal, or a Bible
··· Some symbols from home (family picture, a talisman, special stone, or shell, a sachet of your loved one's perfume or cologne, a small stuffed animal from your young child's menagerie)

When you check into your room, take a moment to set up a little corner for your ritual. Cover the impersonal surface of desk or dresser with a cloth, and arrange your items to enhance a meditative welcome to you when you come in again. If you have a roommate, be as open or discreet as you need to be to be comfortable.

When you return to your room at the end of a day, give yourself time to unwind. Flip through the channels on television, read over work or materials, call home, or order room service. Then when you are refreshed, light a candle and sit in front of it. Hold the people you love in prayer. Unburden yourself from the day. Read through the order of worship for evening prayers. Look at the day's lectionary passages. Pick one (be realistic!). Read through it and meditate on it, asking yourself what word or call there is for you this day. It may bring you comfort to know that your family is reading the same prayer or scripture passage, so arrange ahead of time with those left behind to meditate on the lectionary passage or appointed prayer too.

If morning prayer suits you better, save time before your meeting or departure time to greet the day with prayer, readings, or study. The space you have set up will orient you as you wake up in a strange room. The symbols remind you of who you are and whose you are, no matter where you go.

LIFE TRANSITIONS

· · · · · · · · · · · ·

ℬ𝒾𝓇𝓉𝒽

BIRTH PRAYERS

God of all creation, we are in awe this day at the mysterious wonder of your divine power. We are honored to be partners with you in the creation of this child. In the birth of this tiny one we can see the mark of your hand. With tears of joy and hearts overflowing with gratitude, we give you praise and thanksgiving for the gift of *(name of child)*. May *(he/she)* be kept safe within your sheltering arms. May *(he/she)* be guided by your path of righteousness. May *(he/she)* grow in the knowledge and love of Christ. Amen.

—

Mothering God, you know the pain and joy of birthing labor. From your womb comes forth all of creation. We celebrate with joy the birth of *(name of child)*. We give you thanks for a safe and healthy delivery for both *(names of mother and child)*. We give you thanks for the steadfast presence of *(name of father)*. We give you thanks for the skill and gifts of those attending this birth. We know your hand guided this journey of birth from womb to world. Bless this child and guide *(him/her)* in *(his/her)* new journey of life. Bless *(names of mother and father)* as they seek your wisdom in raising *(name of child)*. Bless *(names of other family members)* as they receive *(name of child)* into their family. In the name of your beloved child, Jesus of Nazareth, we pray. Amen.

—

God of power and mystery, in the birth of this child we have experienced the pain and joy of creation. We give you thanks that the struggle of birthing is over. We give thanks for the life of *(name of child)*. Bless *(name of child)* with your gracious countenance. Surround *(him/her)* with your loving and protective arms. Bless *(names of parents)* with your continued guidance. Give them strength and hope in the task of parenting. May they know they are surrounded by others with whom they can seek support and care. Bless this family. Be ever present in their journey of life together. In the name of the crucified and risen one, Jesus Christ, we pray. Amen.

Sometimes in birth, a tragedy occurs. The death of a newborn or a miscarriage is one of the most difficult experiences in life. It is a time to seek God's presence.

PRAYER FOR A STILLBIRTH

O God, there is an aching in us. We turn to you for comfort, for answers, even for a way to raise our fists to heaven. Help us through our sorrow and our questions and our anger. Help us to name our feelings. Consecrate the memory of this child *(call the child by name if possible)*. Be with us in the empty space that haunts us. We pray in the name of Christ, who knew suffering and sorrow. Amen.

The family may wish to gather and light a candle purchased to commemorate the day. People may feel moved to talk about their disappointments, their relief, their confusion, their sadness. If a name had been picked out for the time of birth, you may offer the name in prayer. It is important to acknowledge the emptiness that you may be feeling. If on subsequent anniversaries of the date you wish to light the candle and say a prayer again, you may make that a family event. We need to remember that the fabric of life has this kind of texture, with sorrow and loss woven right in next to joy and celebration. Liturgy can speak our sighs as well as our songs.

PRAYER FOR A MISCARRIAGE

O God, the loss and sudden surprise are overwhelming. Strengthen us in this hollow time. Give us words to name this silent, private experience. Then sit with us in our silence and our sorrow as we realize the passing of hope. We pray in the name of Christ, who is our hope. Amen.

Adoption

When a child or several children are adopted into a family, it is a time of great joy and celebration. It is an appropriate occasion in the life of a family to have this time of transition recognized within the community of faith. Some churches may have a liturgy for the celebration of adoption to be used during a worship service. Families may want to consider having a celebration in their home to recognize, affirm, and celebrate the adoption. Such a celebration might include a special meal, gifts for the family or newly adopted child, and symbols to recognize this important step in a family's life. A Christ candle can be lit prior to offering a prayer. Along with the Christ candle, consider having one candle for each member of the family. Light the Christ candle first. Then light each family member's candle from the Christ candle, naming the family member as the candle is lit.

Gracious God, who has chosen us to be your people, we give you thanks that you have chosen and given to us *(name of adopted child or children)*. Bless *(name of adopted child)* as *(he/she)* grows in understanding of what it means to be a member of this family. May *(name of parent or parents)* seek your guidance and wisdom in parenting. Help *(names of siblings or other family members)* to grow in their love and acceptance of *(name of adopted child)* as a member of this family. May your compassionate and gracious presence be with us as we journey together in life. In the name of our Savior and brother, Jesus the Christ. Amen.

— or —

God, you are like a mother and a father to us, and we are your chosen children. With grateful hearts we give you thanks for the gift of *(name of adopted child or children)* to this family. May the security of unconditional love, the comforts of a safe home, and the deep companionship of caring individuals be made known to *(name of adopted child or children)*. In joys and struggles, be with us, gracious Creator, as we explore together what it means to be a family. May your steadfast love, unending grace, and constant presence abide with us and serve as a model for our life together. In the name of your chosen one, Jesus the Christ. Amen.

Birthday

There are many ways to celebrate birthdays, some of which have a life and momentum of their own, carrying us along in a tide of commercialism and consumerism. From pizza parlor to roller-skating rink, replete with goody bags and plastic cake decorations, birthdays get a lot of attention. Spending some centering time at home to remember who we are and whose we are is important for these special celebrations. Try these ideas, and add your own family traditions and prayers.

• BIRTHDAY CELEBRATION OF THANKSGIVING •

Make a chain of thanksgiving. You will need to prepare strips of construction paper, and have markers and tape or glue available. On each strip write something about the celebrant's life for which you are thankful. Everybody may write something on the links, or one person may fill them all out. Link the strips of paper in a chain representing the number of years being celebrated. Loop the chain around the birthday cake or Christ candle, or hang it around the room if the links add up to a long chain. Light the Christ candle before lighting the candles on the birthday cake.

Pray: **Christ gives us abundant life. Christ reminds us who we are. Thanks be to God for new life in Jesus Christ! Amen.**

After the traditional birthday cake candles have been blown out, or the "Happy Birthday" chorus sung, have the celebrant tear off a ring at a time. Read aloud the things for which you are thankful, and let the family members add an "Amen!" or a "Thank you, God!" or embellish the story with great relish and detail.

WALL OF HONOR LITURGY

Make a "wall of honor." Cover a kitchen bulletin board or the wall of a central gathering area with birthday wrapping paper. Put up photographs of the birthday honoree; include snapshots representing various stages of life. You may also pin up meaningful memorabilia, such as awards, confirmation certificate, concert programs, drawings, church school projects, baby booties, and letters. Festoon the board with ribbons or crepe paper. When family members are gathered, encourage individuals to pick a photo or symbol and recall a story about the birthday celebrant. As the storytelling winds down, light the Christ candle and read the story of Jesus' birth in Matthew or Luke.

Pray: **Great and loving God, when you birthed your Son, Jesus, in humble surroundings in Bethlehem, you made noble all of our births. As we celebrate *(name's)* birthday, we celebrate all that is Christlike in *(her/him)*. Help *(name)* to walk in Christ's way throughout life. We pray in the name of Jesus, our brother. Amen.**

BIRTHDAY PRAYERS AND BLESSINGS

God, today we celebrate the birthday of *(name of person)* with fun, feasting, and gifts. This is one of the best days in the year! Be with us in our joy. Bless *(name)* and all who celebrate with *(her/him)* today. Join with us as we rejoice in *(name's)* special day and sing "Happy Birthday." Amen.

—

Giver of life, we give thanks this day for *(name of person)*. *(She/He)* is truly a gift of joy in our lives. Be present with us in our celebration this day. Continue to bless *(name)* with your divine presence. May you guide and direct *(her/him)* in the years ahead. May you grant *(her/him)* a healthy, strong life. May you give *(her/him)* courage and strength in times of struggle. May *(she/he)* always know that deep within *(her/him)* lies your divine image. In the name of your chosen child, Jesus the Christ, we pray. Amen.

—

Holy Creator, come and dance among us this day as we celebrate *(name's)* birthday. Above all other days, may we recognize with joy on this special day the gift you have given us in *(name)*. Bless us all with your presence at our party. Bless *(name)* that *(she/he)* continues to grow in grace and truth as one of your servants. Amen.

A Prayer for a Special Birthday

Source of all created life, rejoice with us this day as we gather to celebrate *(name of person and his/her number of years)*. All birthdays are important, but today marks a special milestone in *(name's)* journey. We give you thanks for having guided *(name)* to this point. We remember the day of *(her/his)* birth and all the subsequent birthday celebrations. We give you thanks for the joy and delight that *(she/he)* gives to us and to others. We are gifted by *(her/his)* presence in this world. Bless *(her/him)* this day. Grant *(her/him)* your continued presence, guidance, and wisdom in the years to come. May *(she/he)* discover more fully the gifts you have bestowed upon *(her/him)*. Allow these gifts of your Spirit to be used for *(her/his)* delight and in your service. May *(name)* always know of your deep and abiding love for *(her/him)*. In the name of Christ, we pray. Amen.

Confirmation

Confirmation is a rite of the church in which individuals baptized as infants or children affirm the baptism vows taken on their behalf. It is a time of transition that recognizes an individual's personal responsibility for Christian discipleship. Most often adolescents are involved in the confirmation process. The confirmation process includes an examination of the Christian faith and discipleship of Christ. After completing the process, and after having been approved by the local congregation, individuals are confirmed. Confirmation may also signify mature membership responsibilities in the church. The rite of confirmation takes place before the congregation during worship.

Invite relatives and friends to celebrate confirmation in your home. Remember to include those who have helped to nurture the newly confirmed member in the faith (church school teachers, youth leaders, etc.). Plan a special meal and include favorite foods of the newly confirmed person. If gifts are given to the newly confirmed person, encourage gifts that reflect the nature of the occasion, such as books of inspiration, prayer, or meditation, family heirlooms, or a gift to a special mission in honor of the confirmand. Consider having people write letters to the confirmand. These letters can include comments on how they have seen the person mature, thoughts on the importance of the Christian faith in the lives of those writing, hopes and blessings for the honored person, among other things. Gather these letters into a notebook.

Consider making a special loaf of bread to serve with the meal. Include a Christ candle or the confirmed individual's baptismal candle on the table. Light the candles before the meal or blessing. Keep them lit throughout the celebration. Decorate with pictures and mementos of the honored person's baptism. Offer a special prayer or blessings for the confirmand. A favorite scripture can be included. The honored confirmand can also offer a prayer thanking those who have served as mentors and guides in the faith.

A CONFIRMATION BLESSING

God of all wisdom and truth, with great joy we celebrate today the confirmation of *(name's)* baptism vows. We thank you for having guided *(him/her)* to this decision. We give thanks for all those who have nurtured *(name)* in the Christian faith. We ask that your presence and counsel continue to direct *(name's)* journey of life and faith. May *(he/she)* always know of your steadfast love and abundant grace. May the gifts of the Spirit that you have given to *(name)* be used to further the ministry of Christ in all the world. The love of God, the grace of our Savior, Jesus Christ, and the power of the Holy Spirit be with *(name)* and all of us gathered in this place. Amen.

A CONFIRMATION TABLE LITURGY

Reader: We are gathered to celebrate the confirmation of *(name of person)*. We begin our celebration by lighting a candle(s) to remind us of the presence of Christ in our midst.

(Light a Christ candle, the confirmand's baptismal or confirmation candle, or other candles.)

Read: *(Read one of the following or a favorite verse of the newly confirmed person: Psalm 119:97–106; Ephesians 4:1–6, 11–13; 6:10–17; Colossians 3:12–17; 1 Peter 2:9–10.)*

Pray: God who calls us to be your servants, we give thanks for the life, baptism, and confirmation of *(name)*. You have called and guided *(her/him)* to be one of your people. *(She/He)* has accepted your call to Christian discipleship. May your presence continue to guide and protect *(name)*. Give *(her/him)* strength to witness to the faith. May the gifts you have bestowed on *(name)* be used to serve Christ. We give thanks for those gathered here to celebrate *(name's)* confirmation. Bless and keep all of us in your care. For all the gifts of this table, and for our life together, we give thanks. Amen.

La Quinceañera

La Quinceañera is a special celebration held in many Spanish-speaking cultures for young girls when they reach the age of fifteen. This celebration marks the girl's entrance into womanhood. It is quite a festive celebration. Friends and family gather together to celebrate the young girl's *quince años,* or fifteenth birthday. The festivities begin with a special service held at church. The honored girl wears white and is escorted to the church with great fanfare. Her friends may serve as attendants at the worship. Following worship, a reception is held. In some families a daughter's *quince años* is honored with a special gift or trip rather than a party. In either case, this special birthday marks the entrance of a young girl into a new phase of her life.

PRAYER

Gracious Companion and Giver of life, you were present at *(name's)* birth. You have been ever present in her childhood. As she celebrates her fifteenth birthday, we ask for your presence and your blessing of this celebration.

We give thanks for those who have helped her reach this milestone. For parents who have sheltered, nourished, and cared for *(name)* with unending love. For family and friends who have shared *(name's)* joys and struggles, and been companions along the road to this day.

As *(name)* enters into a new phase of her lifelong journey, we ask for your continued presence to guide her into adulthood. It is not an easy journey ahead, but it is one filled with great possibilities and potential. Grant her your blessing for the years to come.

As *(name)* continues to mature, may she realize the gifts within her that your Spirit has given her. May she listen to and grow strong in your wisdom. May she always remember that she is made in your divine image. May her life's journey be filled with joy and surrounded by your infinite love. In the name of Christ we pray. Amen.

LA QUINCEAÑERA TABLE LITURGY

(Prepare favorite foods of the honored girl. Use pictures from her childhood and other memorabilia to decorate the area. Begin the liturgy by lighting a Christ candle.)

Read:
>Today we celebrate *(name's) quince años,* or fifteenth birthday. We recognize that *(name)* is leaving childhood and approaching womanhood. We rejoice with her in this passage. As always we call upon the presence of God in Christ to be with us in our revelry and recognition of *(name's)* birthday.

Read:
>*(Read a favorite scripture of the honored girl or one chosen by her family, or tell a story of one of the great women of the Bible.)*

Share:
>*(Encourage persons gathered to share stories and observations about, and wishes for, the honored girl.)*

Pray:
>**Nurturing God, you have given us birth, and you journey with us our whole lives. Today we ask your blessing upon *(name)* as she celebrates her fifteenth birthday. Today we recognize that *(name)* is becoming a young woman. You, who have guided her in her early years, now be with her in the years ahead as her life unfolds. Help her to realize the beauty that is within her, a beauty that comes from being a reflection of your image. As *(name)* matures, may she seek your wisdom, a wisdom brought to incarnation in Jesus. Make her strong and courageous to face the many challenges ahead. May she use the gifts with which your Spirit has empowered her on behalf of Christ. Fill her life with joy and love. Bless *(name)* all the days of her life. Amen.**

Graduation

PRAYER FOR THE GRADUATE

Source of all knowledge and truth, we celebrate the accomplishments and graduation of *(name)* from *(name of school)*. We give you thanks for *(her/his)* presence in our lives. We give you thanks for parents, teachers, mentors, family, and friends who have helped to nurture *(name)* to this point in *(her/his)* life's journey. We thank you for the many gifts you have given *(her/him)*. May *(he/she)* use the knowledge *(he/she)* has acquired and the gifts *(he/she)* has been blessed with to serve and honor you.

As *(name)* embarks on a new path of discovery, may your continuing and comforting presence be with *(her/him)*. In times of fear, may you bring courage. In times of doubt, may you bring hope. In times of weariness, may you bring strength. In times of struggle, may you bring peace. In times of discernment, may you bring wisdom. In all things may *(name)* seek to follow your way. In the name of Jesus Christ, who is your Word and Wisdom made flesh, we pray. Amen.

BLESSING LITANY FOR THE GRADUATE

*(Invite those gathered to offer prayers on behalf of the person who is graduating. After each petition, have those gathered respond: "Bless (name), O God."
Read the following to begin and then to end the litany. You may want to form a circle around the graduate. Consider having those gathered put their hands on the head of the graduate as you pray. Light a Christ candle before you begin the blessing.)*

Read: God of all wisdom and truth, we are here to celebrate the graduation of *(name)*. We give you thanks for *(name's)* presence among us. We give you thanks for the joy *(she/he)* brings to our lives. We give you thanks for *(her/his)* accomplishments. We ask your blessing be with *(her/him)*. Hear our prayers for *(name)*.

(Those gathered offer prayer for the graduate. After the petitions for the graduate have come to a close, end the prayer with the following.)

Gracious God, we ask that you receive all these prayers and blessings for *(name)*. Keep *(her/him)* in your tender care. Guide *(her/him)* along the path of righteousness. Surround *(her/him)* with your love. In all things may *(name)* follow the way of Christ, the way of compassionate and boundless grace. Amen.

Wedding

Pray: Gracious God, we ask your blessings this day upon *(names of couple)* as, together with your Holy Spirit, they establish this covenant of marriage. Be present in the love that they share so that they might come to know the miracle of two lives become truly one. Lift them to heights of joy that, until this day, have been only glimpsed. Allow them to live for each other. Sustain them in times of testing that the eternal nature of your love may be a source of strength in the life that now opens before them. Bless the rings they give to each other that they might be signs to all of creation of the love made possible through your presence. Allow these two, O God, to know the gifts of community made visible through our gathering this day and in those whose hearts gather with us through the power of your Holy Spirit. May their burdens always be shared, and may their joys ever be magnified for we ask it in the name of our Sovereign and Savior, Jesus Christ. Amen.

Wedding Anniversary

Consider reading the scripture that was read at the couple's wedding before using one of these prayers.

Holy Companion, today we remember the marriage of *(names of couple)*. They have been married for *(number of years)*. We give thanks that you have blessed and guided their relationship. We ask your blessing today and in the years ahead. May their love continue to deepen, may their respect for each other expand, and may their journey together be filled with more joy than tears. We pray in the name of the one who exemplified your love, Jesus Christ. Amen.

– or –

God of covenant and promise, we celebrate today the marriage covenant made between *(names of couple)*. For *(number of years)* they have kept their promises to each other and you. Their commitment to each other has been a blessing and joy to friends and family alike. We give thanks for the home they have created together. A home where mutual respect and trust are demonstrated; where grace and forgiveness abound; where the meaning of sacrificial love and service to others is modeled; where joy is deep and pain is shared. A home that serves as an example of your call to covenantal living. We give thanks for your continued presence in their lives. You are at the heart of their life together. You have seen them through pain and tears, through laughter and delight. Bless and guide their journey ahead as you have blessed and guided their past. May the light of their love continue to radiate to others as a beacon of your enduring love. In the name of Christ we pray. Amen.

– or –

God of enduring love, we give thanks to you for *(names of couple)*, and the marriage they share. In a world where so much seems disposable and human relationships expendable, their marriage provides an example of mutual respect, endurance, and fidelity. We give thanks for the home they have made together. A home where love, grace, and forgiveness abound; where hurt and brokenness are mended. A home where sacrificial love is made apparent; where children have been born and raised to be loving and compassionate. A home where hospitality abounds and visitors are made to feel welcome. Continue to be present and bless *(names of couple)*, O God. May future years be as rich and fulfilling as the past ones. In the name of Christ, we pray. Amen.

Blessing for a New Home

Pray:

O God, you have been our dwelling place for all generations. May this house become a place for your Spirit to dwell. May the walls encompass a home that is filled with unending love and laughter. May those who live within this shelter find a nurturing place for the growth of both body and spirit, a safe place to be sheltered from the brokenness of the world, a healing place to find respite from the stress of daily life, a teaching place where the lessons of faith are taught and lived, a loving place where forgiveness and grace permeate the relationship of those living together as family. Come, Holy Spirit, bless this dwelling place and all those who now abide within it. Amen.

— or —

Ever present God, whose home is the heavens and earth and all therein, come and bless this new home. Bless each room of this *(house/apartment)*, the kitchen where meals are prepared, the living room where play and work are centered, the bedrooms where peaceful rest is given for daily renewal, the bathroom where bodies are cleansed. Bless those who live here, *(names of individuals)*. May they remember that a home is built more on love and faith than on brick and mortar, wood and nails. May anger dissipate quickly and joy and laughter abide generously. Grant your blessing to each one living within these walls. May this home become a place where faithful discipleship is nurtured. In the name of Jesus the Christ. Amen.

A Liturgy for a New Home

(Invite friends and family to this celebration. This liturgy is designed to be followed by a meal. It may be appropriate to ask those who have come for this celebration to contribute to the meal. A candle may be used on the table to signify the presence of Christ.)

Read: Welcome to our new home. It is with joy that we have you as our guests to celebrate this new beginning in our lives and to ask God to bless our new home.

Read: *(Read Psalm 90:1–2, 127:1–2, or 139:1–2.)*

Pray: O gracious God, we give you thanks for this new home. Throughout history you have made known your presence to your people whenever they have journeyed and made a home. We ask that you grace this home with your abiding presence. Bless this house, its walls, and its floors that give us a place to have safe shelter from the world. May its door serve as a threshold of peace and wholeness for those entering. Help us to see that a home is not so much a place as a way of living with one another.

     May those who live in this place be anchored in your steadfast love. May joy, respect, forgiveness, and grace abound among those living here. May guests find gracious hospitality and a welcoming presence. May the door of this home always be open to others. May the divine presence of Christ that graced so many feasts in our past be with us this day in our celebration of this new home. Amen.

(Optional: You may want to sing an appropriate hymn or certain stanzas of a hymn such as "For the Beauty of the Earth" or "Now Thank We All Our God.")

Moving

We live in a mobile world. We may move several times in the course of our lives. The moves may be across a city, across the country, or across the world. Moving from one place to another is a major event in our lives. It is a time filled with excitement, apprehension, and sadness.

PRAYERS BEFORE MOVING

God of the traveler, since Abraham and Sarah, you have moved with your people. Be with us now as we move from one place to another, from one home to another, and from one job to another. It is a difficult and daring adventure. We are excited and frightened by the possibilities that lie ahead. As we pack up our belongings, help us to pack up our fears. Grant us courage for all the newness that we will encounter. Give us strength to say goodbye to family and friends. May we find joy in our new home and friends among strangers. Go before us, as you did for our ancestors in the wilderness. Guide us with your fire of love and your cloud of presence. In the name of Jesus, our Savior and companion along the way. Amen.

—

God of the Exodus, you delivered Moses and Miriam and the Hebrew people as they crossed the Red Sea. You led your people as they murmured and complained about bitter conditions in the wilderness. You delivered your Son from his wilderness and walked with him in his ministry. Now, we call upon you. Help us to cross over into a new land. Ease the bumps of transition. Iron out the wrinkles resulting from too tightly packed days and too hastily packed boxes. Make us aware of Christ's presence in our midst—in the faces of friends and strangers, in the challenge of adjustment, in the excitement of a new place to call home. We will keep you in our hearts as we move. We pray that you will hold us in your heart, too. Amen.

CELEBRATION FOR MOVING

Encourage each member of the family to rescue from the packing process a small significant possession. Just before you are ready to leave the old space, collect these favorite possessions and parade through the home with them. If you still have a Christ candle out, someone can lead the way with it. When the little pilgrimage is over, gather in a circle and say a prayer similar to this:

God was in our midst here, through good times and bad. God will go with us to be in our new home and help us with the rough spots and the new joys. Thank you, God, for your constant presence. Bless us and our chosen treasures as we make this passage into a new home. Amen.

When you arrive in your new home, repeat this process with your chosen treasures. Say a prayer like this:

O God, our true home and our best hope, we know that you are not confined to one place. We know that our possessions do not define who we are. Yet in this time of transition we hold on to something familiar even as we look to you for a sense of home and identity. Stay with us, we pray, in Christ's name. Amen.

PRAYER AFTER MOVING

We are here! Thank you, God, for a safe journey. As we begin a new life, help us to make this place our home. May we find people to trust and to care for us. May we find our work rewarding. May we find good places to meet people, to worship, to shop, to go to school, and to play. Dwell with us in this new place as you do in all places that we find ourselves. As we set about unpacking, enable us to open up to the newness around us. In the name of Jesus, whose home in our hearts, we pray. Amen.

Divorce

Divorce is a difficult time of transition for couples, children, and families. A covenant has been broken. But in the midst of this brokenness God's care and love are steadfast. In this time of struggle it is important that we call upon God to be with us, to forgive us, and to help us move forward. Children especially need to be reassured that they bear no cause for the divorce, and that God's love and presence abide with them. If possible, have both parents and children gather to say a prayer and have a closing liturgy. This ritual is helpful in finalizing the divorce as well as helping those involved move forward in new relationships with one another.

PRAYER OF REPENTANCE, FORGIVENESS, AND HOPE

God of promises, we come to you with heavy hearts and shattered spirits. The covenant of marriage made before you has been broken. It cannot be repaired. Words and actions have not reflected your grace and compassion. In this struggle we have been angry, hurt, and despairing. We ask your forgiveness for our inability to continue in that relationship. Forgive us, *(names of marriage partners)*. Help us remember that when we open our hearts in confession, you have promised the grace of your forgiveness. We do not know what form that will take, but we pray that you will make us open to your healing Spirit in our lives.

Be with all of us as we move ahead to a new way of living. Be especially with *(names of children)*. Assure them that they are continually loved by you, by their parents, and by their extended family. Help them to realize they have not contributed to the brokenness around them. They are gifts of joy from you.

Take away our anger and hurt. Restore joy to our hearts. Make our spirits whole. Guide us in the paths ahead. When we are alone, remind us of your presence and the presence in our lives of those who love us. Move us toward new kinds of relationships with one another. Grant us your peace. Amen.

LITURGY OF PARTING

(The divorcing couple, the children, and any other family members may gather together around a table. Have a Christ candle on the table. Consider sharing a meal before or after the liturgy of parting.)

Read: We light the Christ candle to remind us that the love of God, the grace of Christ, and the comforting power of the Holy Spirit are present with us. Although human relationships end, God's love is steadfast and everlasting.

(Light the Christ candle.)

Read: We are here to say goodbye to one way of living. We are here to acknowledge our grief and pain at the ending of this marriage. We are here to ask forgiveness for our inability to continue in a marriage covenant. We are here to reassure one another that God's care and love for us do not end. We are here to ask God's help in beginning a new way of living. As parents and family members, we are here to proclaim to (names of children) that our love for them has not changed.

Read: Hear these words from Scripture. *(Read one of the following: Psalm 42 or 130; Isaiah 55:6–13.)*

Pray: Eternal Covenant Partner, we come before you in sadness and relief. The marriage of *(names of marriage partners)* has ended. Forgive them for the pain, anger, and grief they have caused each other and their family. Let them put the past behind them. Reassure them of your continued grace and love even now. Give them hope for a the future.

Bless *(names of children)*. Be with them as they readjust to a new way of living with their parents. Let them know of your constant presence and their parents' continued love. Remind them of all those who love and care for them.

Give all gathered here the courage and strength to move ahead, to meet new challenges, and to begin again. Empower us to be gracious and forgiving in our relationships with one another. Help us to keep our commitments and responsibilities to one another. Guide us in the journey ahead. Grant us your peace. In the name of Jesus Christ, our Savior, the one in whom all things are reconciled to you. Amen.

(Or you may conclude by having those present say the Prayer of Jesus together.)

Times of Vocational Change

Leading meaningful and productive lives is an important aspect of life's journey. In any vocation there are change and challenges. These challenges affect not only the individual, but also family and coworkers. Changing responsibilities, relocating, moving from job to job, getting promotions, losing employment, and failing to receive recognition at work are only some of the changes that affect our lives. Since it is God's call that brings us to any vocation, it is to God we turn in times of vocational transitions.

FOR A NEW OR BEGINNING VOCATION

God who calls us into life, we give thanks for calling *(name)* to this vocational position. Guide *(name)* as *(he/she)* begins the new responsibilities and tasks required by this work. May *(he/she)* use the gifts with which you have empowered *(him/her)* in a meaningful way. May *(he/she)* meet challenges with grace. May *((he/she)* find joy in this occupation. May *(he/she)* remember that *(his/her)* true vocation is one of faithful discipleship. And to that end, may all *(he/she)* does serve Christ. Amen.

FOR A CHANGE IN POSITION

Holy Creator, you call us to live within a world that is constantly changing. Give us the courage to face these dynamic challenges. Help us through this change. If we or others have been hurt by changes in job positions, be present in this time of disappointment and hurt. Help us to be gracious and compassionate in our relationships with others in the workplace. Give us the skills to accomplish the tasks at hand. Remind us that in whatever work we do, we are called to be your servants. Amen.

LOSS OF EMPLOYMENT

God who hears our crying, hear us now. We are angry, hurt, and frightened about the future. We have lost not only a task but also a livelihood. Some of our dignity and self-worth has been taken away. We are bewildered and feel hopeless. Through the ages you have been with your people in wilderness. Be with us in this time of wilderness. Guide our steps. Give us courage and determination. Restore our hope. Enfold us in your ever present love. Let us be receptive to the help and love of family and friends, for they reflect your care for us. In the name of Jesus Christ, our Savior. Amen.

RETIREMENT

Retirement in years past seemed a clearly divided line between the old world and the new. This passage from one stage of vocation to another has changed. More people have varied careers or multiple jobs in a lifetime. Many retire from one career and begin active volunteer lives, become consultants, or discover some of the joys of creativity at home. This transition is truly a birth to a new kind of life. Take time to celebrate.

Your celebration may include a special meal with friends, coworkers, and family. Singing songs such as "Thuma Mina" (Send Me), "Kum Ba Yah," "Be Thou My Vision," "Here I Am, Lord," and "I Was There to Hear Your Borning Cry" may be a significant part of the celebration. You may want to decorate a hat or wreath with symbols of the honoree's vocation and hobbies, as well as hopes and well wishes for the next stage of life's journey.

If small children are present, they, along with the adults, may find meaning in the reading aloud of *The Runaway Bunny* by Margaret Wise Brown. This book, read in conjunction with Psalm 139:1–12, reinforces God's loving pursuit and protection of us wherever we may go.

The reading of Psalm 23 in this context brings the shepherding image of God to this time of transition. The retiree could be given a staff or a walking stick to remember God's guidance and care. Song settings of the Twenty-third Psalm could be sung as well.

CELEBRATION FOR RETIRING FROM A LIFELONG CAREER IN ONE PLACE

Prepare: In the center of the family meal table, place a variety of symbols representing the work the individual has done (e.g,. small farm implements, sketch pad, bus schedule, lunch box, uniform, photographs, identification badges, books).

Storytelling:	Begin with each member of the family, including the retiree, sharing a memory from the time of work.
Visioning:	Ask the retiree to share some vision of the coming phase of life. Include whimsical dreams as well as practical schemes. *(Invite people to join in a litany prayer. After each petition, invite those gathered to say the response.)*
Pray:	Holy Worker, for all the memories of days gone by, for colleagues fair and frustrating, for all the stretching moments of learning and adjusting and discovering,
Response:	We give you thanks, O God.
Pray:	For the familiar smells of work, the comforting feel of the same chair, the various pitches of coworkers' voices, the memorable taste of cafeteria food, the furtive glances at the clock,
Response:	We give you thanks, O God.
Pray:	For dreams of a new way of being, for health and pleasure in the coming years, for a vision of creative ways to use gifts,
Response:	We ask your help, O God.
Pray:	For patience as we find new patterns, for healing of old wounds, for wisdom to close one chapter and open another,
Response:	We ask your help, O God.
Pray:	All this we ask in the name of the One who reminds us who we are at all times of our lives, the Christ who walks with us and walks before us. Amen.

PRAYER OF THE RETIREE

The one who is about to retire prays the following:

O Shaper of life, you have made me who I am. I am more than a uniform, more than a salary, for I have my life in you. Help me through this passageway. Shape me into a form that fits these twists and turns. And all the way, whisper to me again that I am yours. Amen.

RECOGNITION OF A HOMEMAKER'S LIFELONG CAREER

Use this prayer to recognize the work of a lifelong homemaker. Gather together family members and friends to celebrate this vocation. Prepare a meal of favorite foods of the honoree. Pray this litany before the meal.

Pray: We give you thanks, O Light of life, for *(name's)* gifts. For the golden glow of the lamps at twilight, for the smell of breakfast at the break of dawn.

Response: We remember and give thanks.

Pray: We are grateful, O Weaver, for the stories woven together in this place. For photo albums carefully kept, and tales recounted on birthdays. For scrapbooks lovingly pasted together and the warm blanket of memories of being tucked in at night with a bedtime story.

Response: We remember and give thanks.

Pray: We lift up with laughter and love, O Creator, the memories of costumes that didn't work out, cakes that fell, creations that fell short of *(name's)* dreams.

Response: Hear our prayers and our memories.

Pray: We may not have known, O Master Builder, of the plans that were never completed, of deferred dreams and unfulfilled longings. If we have been insensitive or selfish,

Response: Hear us now and forgive us.

Pray: We bless your holy name, O Spinner of possibilities. We pray your blessing on *(name)* in the coming season of life. Spin out the possibilities for fulfillment, for discernment, for dreams to be realized and gifts to be celebrated.

Response: We pray and we know we are heard. Amen.

Hospitalization and Treatment

Whether we are going for testing, a simple procedure, surgery, or extended care due to illness, being in a hospital can be a difficult and frightening experience. We need to recognize our uncertainty and fear. We need to call upon God to be with us and persons who are tending to our health care needs.

PRAYER BEFORE ENTERING THE HOSPITAL

Source of life, I am afraid. As I enter this hospital I am fearful of my powerlessness, of the unknown, of pain, of machines and tests, of my lack of knowledge, of news that may come to me.

Be with me. Remind me that you are ever present in my life. Calm the storm of fear that seems to engulf me. Reassure me that those working in this place are those who are called to the vocation of healing. They will care for me. I am not alone. Come, Holy Comforter, and guide me in the time ahead. Amen.

PRAYER BEFORE SURGERY

The reading of Psalm 121 may offer comfort and courage to an individual facing surgery. You may wish to light the Christ candle at home and read the psalm together. You could provide a copy for those sitting in the surgery waiting room.

Prior to the patient's going into surgery, take his or her hand and share a moment of silence, a word of encouragement, a laugh or a story, and a prayer. Try a simple prayer or blessing like one of these:

May God watch over you.
May God guide the hands and direct the wisdom of the
surgeon and staff.
May God give you peace.
Lean on the everlasting arms of God. Amen.

– or –

O God, we trust in your care. Smooth the worries from our brow; soothe our anxious spirits. Wrap us in the comfort of your presence, in Christ's name. Amen.

— or —

We thank you, God, for the marvels of modern medicine, for the skill of doctors and nurses and technicians. Stay with us in this time of need, as we rely on you above all. Amen.

— or —

O God, you are our strength and our song. Sing into us confidence and courage for facing this procedure. Strengthen us for waiting and recovery. We know you are with us. Amen.

PRAYER FOR THOSE PROVIDING HEALTH CARE

Healing God, we ask that your presence be with those who provide health care. May you guide the technicians, nurses, doctors, and all support staff who work in this facility. May they seek your guidance and reflect your compassionate way in all the services they provide. Grant them good judgment, efficient and capable hands, keen eyesight, listening ears, and gentle hearts. We give thanks for their gifts of healing. In the name of the one who heals in your name, Jesus Christ. Amen.

CANCER TREATMENT AND CHEMOTHERAPY

When a course of chemotherapy or radiation is recommended for a period of time, mark progress with a prayer chain. Take Psalm 23 and divide it up so that a phrase or a verse serves as the prayer for that day. Print the phrase on a strip of colored construction paper, linking together all the verses to make a paper chain. Involve children in the creation of the chain. On the day of treatment, rip off one link in the chain and repeat that phrase. The individual undergoing the treatment may want to take the link along and remember the words, breathe them while waiting, and repeat them while being treated. A loved one may take the phrase along to work, joining the patient in prayer. Children may have the phrase tucked in a lunch box to remember what a relative is going through that day. The fragment may be the call to evening prayer or grace before the meal. When the course of treatment is completed, see how well you know this psalm. Try reciting it together as a ritual of closure on this stage of the journey with cancer.

WAITING
Waiting is a constant theme in the treatment of cancer. That time can be filled with leafing through old magazines to numb or distract the mind. It could also be filled with quieting the mind with prayer.

PRAYER BEFORE TREATMENT
O God, give me courage for facing this day.
Be with me in the valley of the shadow of death.
Be here with the staff—technicians, nurses, and doctors.
O God, give my family the strength to wait with me.
I pray in Christ's name. Amen.

COMPANIONS IN TREATMENTS
Being the one who walks alongside a person with cancer can be a daunting responsibility, filled with mixed emotions. Prayers of this sort may be of help.

God, I know that *(name)* needs your healing and care. Stay close and watchful, I pray.

I need your healing too. Some days I erupt with anger; some nights I am chilled with fear. All the while I am trying to offer support and hopefulness. But I cannot do this without you. Stay with me too.

I pray for all who suffer with disease or with fearfulness. Be our refuge and our strength, O God. Amen.

Extended Caregiving

Within the family there may be times of extended caregiving. A chronically ill child, a parent with Alzheimer's, a relative with a disability—all can provide moments of grace and dignity as well as moments of fatigue or even despair. Both the caregivers and the recipients of care need regular reminders of the One who carries us all, who weeps for our pain and dances with our little victories. These liturgies provide a ritual for recognizing God's presence in the midst of the routines of the day.

Celtic prayers of the day remind us that each act of diurnal drudgery is laced with grace. The homemaker prayed as she stirred the fire; the herder prayed as he milked the cow; the walker prayed as she hit the road; the weary pilgrim prayed as he laid his head down to sleep. What routines of your day could be opportunities for prayer?

Consider having music, prayers, and liturgies recorded on a cassette tape. Recorded stories and passages from the Bible, daily prayers, favorite hymns, and quiet music can provide times of quiet meditation for the individual who is ill. In our infirmities there are times we need solitude. But do not let recordings and books take the place of the community of believers gathered to pray and support the ailing individual.

If an individual is confined to one room, create a worship space that is visible day and night. You may set up a table next to a bed or wheelchair. You may create a large wall hanging or construct a shelf at eye level to provide objects for contemplation. Include a cross, a candle (perhaps the family's Christ candle could be kept here), an icon or symbol of faith, photographs of family members, memories of times shared—a shell from the beach, a pine bough from Christmas, a symbol to represent the current season of the church year. Rotate the objects. Ask what the individual would like to have included in the symbols. Leave a light on at night to illuminate the worship space.

Use a daily prayer book with the individual. Pray the scriptures and read with this devotional for beginning and ending the day.

A CLEANSING PRAYER
(This prayer can be adapted to any kind of daily care that needs to be given.)
Keep the Christ candle in a prominent place in the bathroom. At bath time, light the candle. As you wash the one who is receiving care, say a blessing with the rhythm of the cleansing.

May the peace of God, who created you, fill you.
May the love of Christ, who suffered with us, heal you.
May the presence of the Holy Spirit, which lifts you from your pain, be all around you and within you. Amen.

A FAMILY PRAYER
(Light a Christ candle.)
O God, your eye is on the sparrow. Keep your eye fixed on *(name)* as well. Hold *(him/her)* in your tender care. Fill this room with your presence, fill us all with your power, and give us courage to face each day. We pray in the name of Christ, the Shepherd who cares for the sheep. Amen.

PRAYERS FOR CAREGIVERS
The potential for burnout is great when one is providing ongoing care. Time-outs for refreshment are essential to maintain health in the caregiver. So, in addition to arranging for some respite care, or taking time to go to the movies or take a walk, arrange for an appointment with the One who does not grow weary, who will lift you on eagle's wings and set you down in a calm and nurturing place.

O God, you are the One whose love is unconditional. Mine is dependent upon my energy, my irritability, my patience. There are days when I am undone by this task. This is one of those days. Surround me with your love. Fill me with your compassion. Help me to breathe in your healing Spirit so that I may retain my health and wholeness. Refresh me, O God. Amen.

— or —

Holy One, I am awed by the fragile gift of life. Day after day I tend to one of your own. And I am humbled by the responsibility. Help me to touch with reverence, to speak with respect, to move with care in the presence of *(name of the one being cared for)*. Remind me of Christ's passion for the treatment of the sick and the suffering. I yearn to walk in Christ's way. Amen.

— or —

Creator God, each day you brood like a mother over her suffering child. You weep for the planet. You groan with labor at bringing a new day. You smile tenderly at the acts of compassion and charity. Help me to be like you as I bend and clean and call for prescriptions and tend to the needs of *(name of the one being cared for)*. Cultivate in me a clean heart, free of anger or regrets. Nourish me in my caregiving that I might show your love in all that I do. Amen.

Prayer at the end of the day can bring some closure to a task that seems to have no end. You may wish to preface your evening prayer with the opening words of Psalm 141:

> "I call upon you, O God; come quickly to me;
> give ear to my voice when I call to you.
> Let my prayer be counted as incense before you,
> and the lifting up of my hands as an evening sacrifice."

OTHER PSALMS FOR THE CAREGIVER

For times of discouragement, read Psalms 13; 61:1–5; 63; 86:1–7. For times of reflection, read Psalms 23; 34:1–8; 90:1–2; 121. For times of confidence and thanksgiving, read Psalms 92:1–4; 116:1–7.

PRAYERS OF RELEASE

Sometimes a loved one who is waiting to die needs reassurance that those left behind are ready to let go. Often surrender to death involves a fearfulness or anxiety that needs to be named. Those standing at the bedside can provide permission, or release, and a sense of God's peace as they send their loved one into the arms of God.

As you gather at the bedside of a dying friend or relative, you may wish to share stories, prayers, scriptures, regrets, joys, and reconciliation. Even if the one near death is unresponsive, speak clearly and respectfully as if he or she can respond. These words and this prayerful atmosphere are very healing for everyone present.

You may wish to invoke the words of Simeon from the Gospel of Luke. This prayer, called the Nunc Dimittis, was prayed in the context of a blessing of the ancient prophet on the young Jesus. Now we might use it as a sending of a loved one into Christ's presence. The NRSV translation of these verses gives the following sending forth: "Master, now you are dismissing your servant in peace, according to your word; for my eyes have seen your salvation" (Luke 2:29–30).

The reading of a psalm such as Psalm 121 or Psalm 23, or another favorite, helps those gathered to hear ancient words of assurance about the steadfast love of God. You may pray your own prayer for release or reconciliation or use one of the following.

Holy One, we give you thanks for the blessing of life. Now we pray that you will bless _____ with a peaceful death. Help *(him/her)* to let go and rest in your everlasting arms. We pray in Christ's name. Amen.

— or —

O God, we release our loved one, _____, to your care. We did not own *(her/him)*. *(She/he)* was always yours. We cherish the time we shared. Help us to hold on to our memories even as we let go of this life together. We are together in your love. Amen.

— or —

O God, we have unresolved arguments, dangling conversations, and unfulfilled dreams. Help us to make peace with the unfinished quality of life. Help us to lay to rest ancient feuds and unrealized hopes. Center us in this time of release. Give _____ a sense of your comforting presence. Give us a sense of your compassionate care. And give all of us the strength to let go. In Jesus' name. Amen.

— or —

God of the sparrow, make a home for our loved one, _____. Cover us with your comforting wings in our time of sorrow. We pray for an end to suffering, and we long for the final shelter of your peace. We pray in the name of Jesus Christ, who is our peace. Amen.

Death

Death is a part of life. It is perhaps the most difficult transition to face, because we stand in the presence of utter mystery. Read one of the following: Psalms 23; 46:1–3; 61:1—4; 90:1–2; 130; John 11:25–26a; Romans 8:31–39; Revelation 21:1–6.

PRAYERS AT THE DEATH OF A LOVED ONE

God of mystery, God of hope;
At this moment our minds and hearts are flooded with emotions.
We feel the eddy of pain, relief, anger, joy, abandonment, and fulfill-
ment. Anchor us in your love. Comfort us with your Spirit.
Keep us close to you when the whirlpools of doubt or despair
pull us under.
Be our rock and our refuge. Amen.

—

Living God, we are stunned by *(name's)* death.
Help us to stay centered in your promise to care for us.
Guide us through the winding path of details and arrangements.
Consecrate us for the ministry of prayer and storytelling and
remembering.
Fill us with confidence for the difficult days ahead.
In all that we do, remind us that we are yours. Amen.

—

O God, we give you thanks for *(name)*. We pray with confidence that
(her/his) suffering is over and peace is finally realized. Yet even as we
sense relief, our hearts are tender with grief. So be with us, wiping away
our tears and soothing us. Be with all whose lives were touched by
(name). We pray in the name of Christ, who gives life meaning and
takes away some of death's sting. Amen.

The family may wish to light the Christ candle and to sit in silence. After some quiet time, share reflections about the deceased. Tell a story, read a letter from him or her, or find a photograph or favorite memento to put on the table next to the Christ candle. Give yourselves permission to laugh at funny memories, to express remorse over things that were left unsaid, to grieve over unresolved issues, to speak truthfully together. After this phase of the storytelling, close with this simple liturgy:

One Voice: Jesus said, "I am the resurrection and the life."
All: In Christ we find hope in this difficult time.
One Voice: We remember *(name)* and commit *(him/her)* to God's tender care.
All: Thanks be to God.
One Voice: God will not leave us comfortless.
All: So let us go forward with confidence and hope. Amen.

A TIME TO MOURN AND A TIME TO DANCE

This book began with words of wisdom from the third chapter of Ecclesiastes: "For everything there is a season, and a time for every matter under heaven." The writer of Ecclesiastes then winds through the labyrinth of times and seasons of life, birth, death, war, peace, . . .

We too have walked the labyrinth with these liturgies and prayers for your household. We trust that you are finding your way through the maze of your days with more meaning and mindfulness. We can imagine you gathered at the table around the Christ candle, singing, remembering, hoping, and celebrating. We hope that you will be creating your own liturgies as well, and that in your family you will mark together the time to weep and the time to dance!

LIST YOUR FAVORITES AND WRITE YOUR OWN

Here are some pages for you and your household to use in jotting down some of your favorite verses of Scripture, prayers, and blessings. Try your hand at creating prayers and celebrations for important occasions in your life. Go ahead and try. You can do it!

GOODBYE—GO WITH GOD—AND REMEMBER WHO YOU ARE!

· ·

This celebration has come to an end.
We hope you have enjoyed the time together, friend.
We know for every prayer and blessing read,
There is another that needs to be said.
God's people are never done,
Giving thanks for life and journeys begun.
So be on your way and begin anew,
To create times of feasting for many or few.
And as you leave, this blessing carry,
May God be with you in making merry.
In joys and tears, in ups and downs
God's gracious, loving presence abounds.
And as you journey along Christ's way,
Remember, beloved, take time to pray.

ADDITIONAL RESOURCES

· · · · · · · · · · · · · · · · ·

Alberswerth, Roy F., and Deborah Alberswerth Payden. *Talking With Your Child About the Church Year.* Cleveland: United Church Press, 1992.

Bass, Dorothy, ed. *Practicing Our Faith.* San Francisco: Jossey-Bass, 1997.

Edelman, Marian Wright. *Guide My Feet: Prayers and Meditations on Loving and Working with Children.* Boston: Beacon Press, 1995.

Hays, Edward. *Secular Sanctity.* Topeka, Kans.: Forest of Peace Books, Hall Directory, 1984.

Klause, Henriette Anne. *Put Your Heart on Paper: Staying Connected in a Loose Ends World.* New York: Bantam Books, 1995.

Nagel, Myra. *Talking With Your Child About Prayer.* New York: United Church Press, 1990.

Nelson, Gertrude Mueller. *To Dance with God.* New York: Paulist Press, 1986.

The New Century Hymnal. United Church of Christ. Cleveland: The Pilgrim Press, 1995.

Payden, Deborah Alberswerth. *Talking With Your Child About Sacraments and Celebrations.* Cleveland: United Church Press, 1994.

Sadler, Kim Martin, ed. *The Book of Daily Prayer: Morning and Evening.* Cleveland: United Church Press, 1995–1998 (annual).

To Celebrate: Reshaping Holidays and Rites of Passage. Ellwood, Ga.: Alternatives, 1987.

Whitcomb, Holly. *Feasting with God: Adventures in Table Spirituality.* Cleveland: United Church Press, 1996.